THE
SEARCH

An Essential Guide to Finding the Right Spouse

With love

KAYODE KAMSON

The Search:
An Essential Guide to Finding the Right Spouse
Copyright © 2021 by Kayode Kamson

Published by
Sophos Books Ltd.
2 Woodberry Grove
London
N12 0DR
www.publishwithsophos.com

ISBN 978-1-905669-65-3

Cover illustration and design by *Icon Media*
Printed in the United Kingdom

Contents

To the Almighty God,
the Author & Designer of marriage

Appreciation

This work is written in appreciation of my wife and soul mate, Caroline, for her unending love, spirited devotion, and efforts to make our marriage what God ordained it to be. I also appreciate our children—Olatunbosun, Oluwadamilola, Oluwadunni, and Oluwabukola—for their various thought-provoking questions and thoughts concerning the practice of marriage. Their queries about how to find suitable spouses provoked this book.

Several friends have suggested that my critical thoughts on marriage should be documented. They have a special place in my heart for the production of this book. Among them are Dr Biodun Oyelade, Dr Dele Babalola, Pastor Omasan Oritsesan, Hon. Olivia Joseph, Pastor Funso Gbenro, and all the members of *The Disciples*. Our testimonies and discussions on scriptural verses are part of my spring of godly wisdom. I thank you all for your direct and indirect contribution to the production of this book.

This appreciation does not confer any responsibility regarding the content of this book on anyone named or unnamed here. I remain liable for the entire contents of this book.

Preface

In 2016, forty to fifty percent of married couples in the United States were divorced. Earlier in 2014, fifty-three percent of marriages were dissolved. In the same year, nations such as the Czech Republic, Hungary, Spain, and Portugal recorded above sixty percent divorce cases. Marriages in Africa are not faring any better. In every five marriages in Nigeria, two ends in divorce. This situation is the same in Ghana, Kenya, and many other countries. No doubt, divorce has become a major global crisis. The aftereffects of divorce are monumental.

I don't want my children to be a part of these heart-breaking statistics. I pray that my grandchildren, as well as children and the unmarried across the world, won't become victims of broken homes. Their desire for a happy home should not turn sour. I am not the only one that campaigns for successful marriages. Many parents, well-wishers, and unwed do too. We all want marriages that reflect the glory of God.

Sadly, the world sees things differently. The marriage institution has been hijacked and turned into an instrument of torture. Today, many marriages lack peace and joy. Infidelity seems to be the order of the day. Many couples live in fear that their marriage has nosedived. Human and spiritual forces against marriage seem to be on the increase. The saddest part is that many unmarried people are scared of marriage, while others are making ridiculous nuptial contracts. Some of them neither know nor appreciate the essence of marriage.

This situation calls for a proactive response. We have a duty to encourage the young ones to marry their God-given spouses. This is a duty for every well-meaning mentor, parent, guardian, pastor, etc. We must guide and guard them against marital ruin. We can start by encouraging the unmarried to choose right. A bad spouse means trouble, and a troubled marriage is an arena of misfortune. But we can prevent any of these from happening.

This book is written to address the issues that surround marriage. It is a guide, with strong biblical perspective, for the unmarried. It will empower them to make the right marital decisions. It will also enlighten parents and guardians on how to guide the unmarried.

This book will guide those in search of a spouse, and those who are in a relationship. It will steer you towards the right direction. It will also reveal the essential factors that must be considered when choosing who to marry. You will find godly instructions as this book takes you through the entire process of searching for a partner and getting married. Your success is important to me. Therefore, I pray that you will find the strength to adopt godly guidance on marriage.

- Kayode Kamson

1
THE SPIRITUAL DRIVE

I have taught thee in the way of wisdom; I have led thee in right paths. When thou goest, thy steps shall not be straitened; and when thou runnest, thou shalt not stumble. Take fast hold of instruction; let her not go: keep her; for she is thy life. —Proverbs 4:11-13

We live in an age of increasing campaign for personal freedom. We desire the freedom to say and do what we want. The concept of personal freedom sounds enticing. Freedom appeals to our nature: we want to live above control. Freedom enjoys prominence in this new age as many people advocate for personal freedom in the home, church, marriage, at the marketplace, etc. You have probably been encouraged to promote your interest without considering anyone else.

The consequence of this push is an influx of young men and women who want everything to happen their own way. They want to live on their own terms, doing things how they deem best. This sounds great. And most of us want it that way! We want the freedom to fulfil the dictates of our heart. In relevance to this book, freedom means marrying anyone that you want, the way you want, and when you want.

The import of this form of lifestyle is that, for many people, God and their freedom do not mingle together. You probably have heard these: *"What does God have to do with it? What does He have to do with my waking up and going to work? What concerns Him with the colour and style of my clothes? What concerns Him with my desire to rent a house of my choice? You get too spiritual! God this, God that! Look, it is my own choice if I resign from my job and move to a better one. God has given us the brain to do stuff for ourselves, not to run to Him every time!"*

These arguments often sound convincing. God has given us the potential to accomplish great things, but I reject assertions which suggest that we do not need God in any or certain areas of our lives. The notion that we must not consult God before we carry out our heart's desires is not only erroneous but also a perversion of truth. As God's children, every step we take must be sanctioned by God. Our marital journey requires God's direction. We'll get lost without His guidance. We will also grope in the dark like blind men, make bad choices, end up in wrong places, and hit a deadlock if we are not led by God. The entire process of getting married is not exempted from this. Your marital journey must take off with God and in God. Anything short of this is prone to failure!

This book will show you how to achieve a sustainable search in God. But for now, we'll dwell more on why and how God must be in the control seat of your search for a spouse.

Deceptive Thinking

Prophet Jeremiah once declared, *"The heart is deceitful above all things, and desperately wicked: who can know it?"* *(Jeremiah 17:9 KJV)* I wish this assertion excludes you and me, but it does not — unless we do not dwell in this body called flesh. The prophet's claim is that our hearts can deceive us. The heart can lead us into error. It can entice us to embrace lies and make wrong decisions. Our heart can become corrupt and enslaved by inappropriate passions. Our hearts can give in to human and spiritual manipulations. This heart can ride on the wings of empty promises, ignorance, anger, etc. Seeking a suitable spouse with this bounded heart usually does not yield positive results. Many marriages are built on what I call the spiky four Fs of marriage — *foolishness, falsehood, fear, and fantasy.* Ensure that yours is not built on any of them.

As a result of total reliance on the dictates of their heart, many people plunge into life-changing situations. They neither subscribe to God's leading nor seek His preference for their lives. They jet off on their journey without consulting God. These set of people include those who marry without involving God. They do not acknowledge God in all their moves. But we have been forewarned: *"I am the vine, ye are the branches: He that abideth in me, and I in him, the same bringeth forth much fruit: for without me ye can do nothing"* (John 15:5). This verse refers to the children of God. It cautions that failure awaits those who live outside of God's instructions.

Anyone who is without God won't receive lifelines from Him. And such a person won't rely on the wisdom of God. If God is not in our lives, we will suffer losses. If the expression of our personal freedom opposes divine control, we will fail. Living without God ultimately leads to ruins. A spouse whose actions are not governed by God is a marriage wrecker! Likewise is a man or woman who plans to marry without God.

Your marriage cannot succeed without God. Remember that *"There is a way that seemeth right unto a man, but the end thereof are the ways of death"* (Proverbs 14:12). If you are on the cruise of "do-my-own thing without God," you are set for failure. You can't do anything without God. So, handle your marriage the way God wants.

A Rethink of Personal Freedom

From the foregoing, you will notice that I dissociate myself from the concept of freedom that fails to acknowledge God as the Leader of a man's life. I enjoin you to do the same. True freedom comes from knowing God and accepting Jesus Christ as your personal Lord and Saviour. This means freedom from the shackles of flesh or the evil one. It also means being alive to God's choice for your life.

Your personal freedom revolves around embracing God's plan for your life. This includes getting married to the person He has chosen for you and at the time He sets for you. The success of your marriage is important to God. He must direct your choices, and you will fail if you do not follow His directives. On the other hand, no one wants or deserves to fail. And God does not want you to fail either.

Personal freedom is not an occasion to gratify the flesh, but rather an avenue to accept God's choice. Regardless of the chapter of your life right now, allow God to lead you. Let Him be in the driving seat of your search for a spouse. Embrace His will for your marriage. Keep yourself under divine governance, and be sensitive to the Holy Spirit concerning who you should and should not marry.

Guiding Light

*Thus says the Lord who made the
earth, the Lord who formed it to
establish it – the Lord is his name:
Call to Me and I will answer you,
and will tell you great and hidden
things that you have not known.*
Jeremiah 33:2-3 ESV

*Whether therefore ye eat, or drink,
or whatsoever ye do all to the glory
of God, the Father.*
1 Corinthians 10:31

2

CHECK-IN WITH GOD

The young lions suffer want and hunger; but those who seek the Lord lack no good thing.
—Psalm 34:10

Without the leading of God, our affairs will crash. But this is not the script of God for us. He wants us to prosper. He wants our desires to be well-established and yield good results. These can only happen when we put God first. Psalm 34:10 says, *"The young lions suffer want and hunger; but those who seek the Lord lack no good thing."* Ask God to help you because you can only stay on Success Lane if you seek Him.

Your marriage is in the hands of God. And your marriage will be glorious if you strictly follow God's instruction. Beware, the world has its own idea of "if and when" you should marry. The world claims to know how, when, why, who, and where you should marry. It wants to influence your marriage. Governments, with their legal and administrative apparatus, are prepared to take over your conception of marriage. Some European states and the US, for instance, have amplified the definition of marriage to include same-sex cohabitation. Marriage goals have been altered as unrighteous practices are being introduced daily. The unwed are bombarded with misconceptions that make the concept of Christian marriage unappealing. However, you will succeed if you know the truth, and it is only the truth of God that can set you free. (See John 8:32)

There is a place for personal responsibility in our marital journey. We are often responsible for where we find ourselves and who we end up with. Whoever a person marries determines the success or failure of the marriage. Marrying the wrong person, or marrying at a wrong time, has consequences. Seek and hear the voice of God before you step into marriage. Keep to His voice because this is the best way to ward off failure.

God Leads

The good news is that God is ever-present to lead you. His Spirit wants to conduct you into successful living. The Scripture says, "*Trust in the LORD with all your heart, and do not lean on your own understanding. In all your ways acknowledge him, and He will make straight your paths*" (Proverbs 3:5-6). Your marriage is not exempted from this promise of divine security. God wants to guide you to make the right choice. He promised to help you in all your undertakings when He said, "*I will instruct you and teach you in the way you should go; I will counsel you with My eye upon you*" (Psalm 32:8 ESV). This is an assurance that God will guide your marital journey if you turn to Him.

Forget your own calculation as regards marriage. Turn your thoughts to God. Be honest with your fears before Him. Open your heart, and talk to Him. Seek His mind, and you will be better for it. Matthew 7:7 says, "*Ask, and it will be given to you; seek, and you will find; knock, and it will be opened to you.*"

If you act or live without God's leading, you will be hurt. And your search is not an exception to this harsh reality. Start and stay with God if you desire a successful marriage. The wisdom of God will orchestrate your marriage for success. And the teachings of the Holy Spirit will sustain your marriage.

Before you enter the institution of marriage, allow God to walk and work with you because He sees the end from the beginning. Don't keep God out of your plans and actions. Failure and sorrow await those who keep God away from their life. Marriage is a journey with many unpredictable twists and turns. You need the help of the Holy Spirit to sail through successfully. Allow God to handle yours from the very start because "*Except the Lord builds a house, they labour in vain that builds it*" (Psalm 127:1).

The Almighty God is our Maker, and our lives are in His hands. He alone knows our tomorrow. God wants us to prosper and come to our desirable end. Everything about us is important to Him. He wants to lead us until we fulfil our purpose of existence. He wants to guide us into His provision for us. He wants us to achieve great things. These include finding the right spouse that will go through the corridors of life with us.

Our duty is to humbly ask God to help us. We should also believe in Jesus Christ and accept Him as our Lord and Saviour. Seek God for the good of those who will come into your life — spouse, children, grandchildren, in-laws, family friends, etc. Psalm 34:10 affirms that those who seek God will not lack any good thing.

Failure Stroke

Pre-checking with God is not popular with at least four groups of people:

1. Those that do not know God or believe that He exists
2. Those that do not believe in Him as the Supreme God
3. Those that have not accepted Jesus Christ as their personal Lord and Saviour
4. Those with partial and sleazy Christian faith

These individuals frown at the idea of seeking God in marriage. They trust more in the dictates of their senses. They dismiss divine commandment and persist in their own ways. They love to do what pleases them. Don't join them because they don't understand what it means to *"seek first the kingdom of God and His righteousness..."* (Matthew 6:33). They are not prepared to submit to the leading of the Holy Spirit. They may even jeer at those who submit to God.

God's Word demands vital action on your part. Trust God wholeheartedly and do not depend on your own limited ideas (Proverbs 3:5-6). Lean on Him and ask:

"*Lord, who should I marry?*" His answer will pave way for your marital success.

Guiding Light

*Ask, and it will be given to you; seek,
and you will find;
knock, and it will be opened to you*
(Matthew 7:7).

*Fear not, for I am with you; be not
dismayed, for I am your God; I will
strengthen you, I will help you, I will
uphold you with my righteous right
hand*
(Isaiah 41:10).

3
DON'T LOCK OUT YOUR MENTORS

Without counsel, plans fail, but with many advisers they succeed. — Proverbs 15:22 ESV

God often uses people as trees of blessings for us. He keeps us in relationship with those who will help and guide us on our journey. In this chapter, you will learn why you must seek counsel from people.

You want to know what God says about marriage. You want to come into the fullness of God's truth about it. You want to know your place in marriage. You want to know why you should marry, who you should marry, who you should not marry, what makes a successful marriage, where you should marry, how you should marry, and when you should marry. The people whom God has placed your way will counsel you concerning these things and many more. Identify these set of people in your orbit, and learn from them.

Who are your potential helpers in the area of marriage? Who are those that the Lord has appointed to help you? They include your parents, siblings, relatives, friends, teachers, mentors, strangers, neighbours, etc.

Your parents are your first spiritual guides. Talk to them; ask them questions. Tap into their knowledge. Confide in them, and let them know your fears about marriage. I freely discuss marriage with my children and demonstrate, in many ways, that I am interested in their marriage. To put it bluntly, I want them to get it right in marriage. This is part of my fatherly roles in their lives. As a result, I pray continually to God on their marriage. I always speak the truth of God's words to my children. I advise them to follow God's words pertaining to their lives. As I do, there are many other parents who seek the happiness of their children as well. However, should your parents' marriage be unpleasant, don't be discouraged. God has already prepared the right mentors for you. They could be anyone among those listed above. All you have to do is find them and take counsel.

God directs us through His appointed people. He sets us on the path of success through His chosen vessels. These may include your friends. The Bible says that "*as iron sharpens iron, so a man sharpens the countenance of his friend*" (Proverbs 27:17). Your friends are meant to bring joy, enlightenment, and confidence into your life. And you are to do the same. If this quality is missing in your friends, look further. Hence, don't look down on strangers because God can use anyone for you.

"*Where no counsel is, the people fall: but in the multitude of counsellors there is safety*" (Proverbs 11:14). Learn from your mentors. Ask questions and discuss your concerns about marriage with men and women who will not compromise the integrity of God's word. God wants you to succeed. Thus, He has set guides around you. Find and learn from them.

You Are Never Alone

As marriage preparation is going on, some intending couples might feel forlorn, particularly those who have lost their parents. The absence of their parents could create a dearth of support at that critical moment of their lives. It can be quite depressing when those who love and care for you are not there to support you. This is, however, a deception of the evil one. The devil wants you to believe that you are all alone and without help. And it is self-defeating to believe that no one cares enough to help you through life.

The truth is, you are not alone. God is always with you. He said that He will never leave or forsake you (1 Chronicles 28:20). He will not leave you without a guide. God will never leave you without people who will educate you on marriage.

Therefore, it does not matter who has exited your life; God has ordained many others to come your way. Many people around us are a blessing from God. They will watch out for you and watch after you. They will guide you towards what is meant for you.

The right people are Christians. They acknowledge God in all that they do, and they are heaven-focused. They are the channels of blessings who will teach you the criteria for a successful marriage. Build and maintain a good relationship with righteous people. Check your marriage interest with them. The word of God says that *"Where there is no guidance, a people falls, but in an abundance of counsellors there is safety"* (Proverbs 11:14 ESVi). Your marriage plans should not be averse to this biblical admonition. Listen to your mentors; consider their advice on marriage. They might see what you are not seeing. They might know what you do not know. Spiritual discernment is a gift of the Holy Spirit to believers. Its manifestation could be in your parents, pastor, friends, and many others in the house of God. Tap into their gifts, and draw from their knowledge about marriage.

The Big Caution

If you seek facts from ordinary people, or from carnal materials, you will discover that the world has its marriage standard. And the world will attempt to sell its specification to you. Governments seek to control citizens on matters that relate to marriage. They regularly define and redefine the boundaries of marriage. Governments and people, with no recourse to God, have loads of misconception about marriage. Those under the control of worldly standards will recommend when, where, who, how, and why you should marry.

Remember that God's way is different from ours. The worldly way will perish. Human ideas will fail and lead you into error. Hence, pay attention to the foundation of your marriage. Don't be led out of God's choice for your marriage. As you set out on your marital journey, focus on God and your spiritual guides.

Guiding Light

My son, do not forget my teaching, but
let your heart keep my commandments,
for length of days and years of life and
peace they will add to you
(Proverbs 3:2 ESV).

Where there is no guidance, a people falls,
but in an abundance of counsellors there
is safety
(Proverbs 11:14).

4
PRIMARY REALITY OF MARRIAGE

Likewise, husbands, live with your wives in an understanding way, showing honour to the woman as the weaker vessel, since they are heirs with you of the grace of life, so that your prayers may not be hindered. —1 Peter 3:7 ESV

There are six vital marriage assertions that I uphold. They are my deductions from scriptural teachings about marriage. These assertions are indispensable to my wife and me in our thirty years of marriage. They have helped us to stay focused. Other couples, who share these assertions, have achieved great marriages as well. The assertions are:

Marriage is God's concept.

Marriage is God's construct.

Marriage is God-ordained.

Marriage is God-regulated.

Marriage is God's vineyard.

Marriage is accountable to God.

These are six statements of truth. As indicated before,

they summarise key Bible teachings on marriage. They reveal the fundamental reality that marriage is divine. God created marriage; He owns and presides over it. He uses it for His purpose. He blesses generations through it. Because God designed marriage, He sets rules of engagement for anyone who wants to participate in it.

We are required to follow the rules of God about marriage. And that requirement comes with a rich reward. Isaiah 1:19 says, *"If you are willing and obedient you will eat the good of the land."* All married and would-be couples are in for immeasurable blessings. Anyone who disobeys the instructions of God concerning marriage will lose out on God's promises. But those who follow God's dictates shall be rewarded.

Marriage, as a divine property, means it is not like any other social engagement. It is not a mere social activity as the world wants us to believe. It is not a cultural practice or some sort of ancient practice. It is not a game show, where success is a matter of chance, or where failure is an acceptable outcome. Marriage is a spiritual arena. How you step and stay in it determine the outcome. What you do, or don't do, in marriage have consequences upon your life. As a spiritual entity, marriage will influence your posterity. If you are not willing to embrace this reality, back off because marriage is not for you.

My marriage expectations are anchored on the six revelations I shared above. My role as a husband is accountable to God. I believe that God owns my marriage, and He is in charge. My marriage is in His hands; I don't want it anywhere else. And as I delight in these biblical truths, my marriage has direction. I enjoy peace, comfort, and hope for a better future. There is so much joy when you handle the things of God as He wants. He will help you whenever you fumble once He sees the sincerity of your heart. There is nothing so reassuring and at the same time so humbling than to know that you are in God's vineyard, working as an obedient servant. You will be at peace with yourself and your spouse regardless of your challenges. The Bible says that we will know the truth, and the truth will set us free (John 8:32). One truth to embrace is that marriage is not man-made; it is God's property. Marriage must follow God's ordinances for its benefits to manifest.

Like many people, I started out ignorant of many marital truths. I saw my marriage as mine! I wanted it to run how I wanted. But my way was not God's way. I had a marriage paradigm that was totally different from God's construct. The more I wanted my marriage to conform to my desires, the more I got frustrated. It wasn't just working. It bred stress, arguments, and bitterness between Caroline and me. It was apparent that something vital was amiss in our marriage. I was desperate for answers.

After a diligent study of God's word and taking counsel from godly mentors, I realised that my union with my wife belongs to God. My marriage is His, and I am only His worker in it. As a husband, I was meant to follow God's instructions for my marriage. I realised that I needed His daily guidance. It meant that I needed His "marriage manual" to be successful. Psalm 127:1 became more alive to me: *"Except the Lord builds a house, they labour in vain that builds it."* The moment I embraced this truth, I stopped being a master of my marriage. I became a servant of God in marriage. This mindset comes with peace, joy, and love. It reduces burden and stress. It places our focus on God. In my case, this new mindset has brought untold marital blessings for which my wife and I will forever thank God.

The Uncommon Benefits

If you believe in the six statements of truths presented above, you will enjoy the rewards of marriage. You will experience uncommon peace and freedom from fear. You won't walk in error, or wander in wrong quarters, while you search for your spouse. This means that you will not marry the wrong person whose variants will be described later in this book.

Let's face it. Many people enter into marriage without a clear vision of what they are getting into. They simply do not see the most important element of marriage: its divine nature! Your case should be different. You should know what marriage implies from the perspective of its Creator. You should know the basic needs of husbands and wives. You should know if you are ready to be a faithful servant of God as a wife or husband. You should know if you are prepared to fulfil its divine demands. You should also have confidence that you will succeed. To be utterly ignorant of the spiritual essence of marriage is to be ill-equipped for marriage.

As you consider marriage, strengthen your heart in the word of God. Build up yourself on His word. Proverbs 4:5-6 says, *"Get wisdom, get understanding: forget it not; neither decline from the words of my mouth. Forsake her not, and she shall preserve thee: love her, and she shall keep thee."*

Within the context of marriage, this encouragement means godly wisdom is rewarding. It also means that you will understand the concept of marriage, and you won't join faith and fate with the wrong person. You will know, without an iota of doubt, that a marriage that commences without God is bound to collapse. But with godly wisdom, your marriage will be well-established.

Guiding Light

The soul of the sluggard craves and gets nothing,
while the soul of the diligent is richly supplied
(Proverbs 13:4 ESVi).

There is no fear in love, but perfect love casts out
fear. For fear has to do with punishment, and
whoever fears has not been perfected in love
(1 John 4:18 ESVi).

5
MORE REALITIES, MUCH MORE REALITIES

For I know the plans I have for you, declares
the LORD, plans for welfare and not for evil, to
give you a future and a hope.
—Jeremiah 29:11

In addition to the primary reality of marriage, there are
secondary realities of marriage.

1. The Mother of all Journeys

Marriage is the mother of all journeys in life. It is an all-
influencing driver that will drive you to things, places,
and situations beyond your imagination. Your dreams
and aspirations will revolve around your marriage. Your
actions and inactions will have consequences. Simply put,
your spouse and marriage will be your new world. This is
another reason you must marry the right person. Ask
those who are happily married; they will tell you how
marriage has influenced their aspirations and actions.

This reality was reflected in Apostle Paul's
admonition: *"But I would have you without carefulness. He*

that is unmarried careth for the things that belong to the Lord, how he may please the Lord: But he that is married careth for the things that are of the world, how he may please his wife" (1 Corinthians 7:32-33). This is a tough statement, but it drives home the point. In marriage, there is a compulsive drive towards your spouse. The thoughts of your spouse will consume you. It will moderate your way, behaviour, and thoughts. It is called the impact of a wife on her husband's life and vice versa.

Please note that this reality, particularly as described by Apostle Paul above, does not deride marriage. It does, however, raise a caution. Don't allow anyone to take you away from the presence and purpose of God. If your spouse is dedicated to God, your marriage won't pull you away from God.

2. Extended Social Relations

Marriage widens social circles. When you go into marriage, you inherit a new world of people such as parents-in-law, brothers-in-law, sisters-in-law, aunts-in-law, uncles-in-law, friends, etc. You can't ignore your spouse's family members and acquaintances. If this happens, something has seriously gone wrong. And such a marriage cannot be healthy. Marriage comes with people who will become your family members, friends, and acquaintances. It will create new social settings in which you and your spouse have no choice but to operate.

Your new world will demand endless relational

building and adaptations. You will experience delights in some while others may cause frustration. Either way, you must keep calm and enjoy your marriage.

In the summer of 2018, at a Christian wedding ceremony in Newark-on-Trent, UK, the groom's sister came out, during the reception, and said something that I found so emotional. She faced her brother's new wife and said these words to her: "*God has given you to me! You are the big sister I have always secretly wished I had! And I know you are going to be the best big sister anyone can ever have. You are already filling that gap in my life. Checking up on me, discussing girly stuff with me, calling me up while in the university to find out how I was doing. Already I know that you are going to be the elder sister I have always dreamt about...*"

With tears running down her face, she continued, "*I, I am so happy that you are already acting as the big sister I want. The other time I was struggling in a particular module at the university, you jumped in to help me and made sure I passed the course. You took it upon yourself to sit on the phone with me for many hours and many nights to coach me, unknown to my brother and others. You didn't get tired of me. I did very well in the course all because you came into my life and helped me. I just don't have words to say than I love you. I really do!*" And with more tears of joy streaming down her cheeks, she gave this amazing conclusion: "*Today, I don't see you as just a sister-in-law, but as my very own God-given special darling elder sister. One that I have always wanted! You are my sister, and I love you.*"

Marriage is not limited to the person you marry. Once

you are in it, you will inherit other people. You will begin to accommodate strangers, some of who have been around your spouse for a long time, as your new acquaintances or relatives. People you hardly know will suddenly become very important members of your life, influencing your marriage directly or indirectly. Don't struggle with this; it is a marriage reality. Simply trust God to help you relate appropriately with everyone that will come into your life.

3. Socio-cultural and Spiritual Differences

People have varying attitude and beliefs. Marriage exposes you to these diversities as your social frontier widens. It does not matter whether yours is an intercultural or interracial marriage. You will be exposed to differences in your in-laws, spouse's friends, church members, business associates, college mates, etc. You will witness strange practices and ideas. You will find some of them pleasant and easy to relate with. You will also find some of them hostile and difficult to embrace.

We are to act as God wants. This requires you to love both the "lovable" and "unlovable" in-laws. On a general note, God wants us to live in peace with everyone. "*If it is possible on your part, live at peace with everyone,*" says Apostle Paul in Romans 12:18. With the Holy Spirit's leading, you have the ability to live in peace with people. You can have dominion in your marriage. So hold no fears against the reality of meeting new people. However, this reality does not mean that you should go into any kind of wedlock. No. It says the opposite: look before you leap. Consider the home and social network of your potential spouse.

There was a young woman who ran away only a few days after her wedding. Until the night after her wedding, she did not know that her spouse and in-laws were deep in occult practice. She was perturbed by the rituals her husband's grandmother performed, on her wedding night, to welcome her into the family. Two nights later, she was woken up at midnight by three strange-looking men whom her young husband had let into their bedroom. They told her to stand naked before them, and they gave her a substance from a calabash to rub on her body. While she did that, they chanted some incantation. Fortunately, she had the mind to take off the following morning and report this strange initiation to her parents and pastor.

Many of such initiations still exist in nations across the world. They have spiritual connotations; be careful! Know the cultural and religious background of your would-be spouse. Later in this book, we'll discuss how to avoid contrary beliefs and spiritual entanglement in marriage.

4. A Dragnet

Beyond being exposed to problems, one can get caught up in strange practices without a choice. Marriage is like a dragnet that pulls you into many social settings. A notable example is culture. My wife comes from a Nigerian ethnic group that is different from mine in many ways. Her ethnic group has rich cultural practices. When we got married, I found some of these practices amazing, amusing and sometimes outright bizarre. The first thing I noticed was their mode of dressing. Men tie wrappers like women. They love to wear shirts upon wrappers, particularly on important occasions.

In my own culture, it is taboo for men to appear in wrappers in public places. Again, my wife's clan welcomes important guests with a tray of assorted drinks, pieces of kola nuts, and cash gathered from household-members and friends of the host. They will gather around you and take turns to "donate" different sum of money to "support the tray of kola nuts" and drinks. A short welcome speech, in Okpe language, usually follows. Guests are expected to accept the gifts, money, and drinks before any discussion. These practices and many more were strange to me, but I found out that I loved them. On my traditional wedding ceremony, I wore a shirt and tied a wrapper too, publicly.

Similarly, some of the practices in my culture appeared strange to my wife, but not any more. They are now part and parcel of our lives. Interracial and intercultural marriages are dragnets. They expose you to new human values. Some will be comfortable, while some will be uncomfortable. You will be expected to adopt a new language, style, and knowledge. Always remember that your marriage belongs to God. It is His vineyard; it is neither yours nor your spouse's. Only by understanding this can you draw the line at what you accept in marriage.

Some people have a deep affinity towards their culture. if you marry one of them, you must be prepared for occasional misunderstanding. Sometimes, your spouse might find some of your conducts unacceptable, and vice-versa. And this may give rise to conflict.

If your search for a spouse is rooted in God, you will enjoy the differences that come with marriage. You will escape the negative effects of these differences. You won't end up with a spouse that will stand against your marital values. You and your spouse will not embrace unrighteous rites prescribed by socio-cultural background.

5. Daily Changes

In marriage, you will grow old. Many people don't like to think about this, but it is a vital factor. Getting old in marriage means your physical appearance is bound to change. The changes are rapid in some people and gradual in others. The beautiful face and athletic body will age and wrinkle. The Bible affirms this when it says, "*All flesh is like grass and all its glory like the flower of grass. The grass withers, and the flower falls…*" (1Peter 1:24) All flesh, with its beauty and glory, will grow old. We might strive to maintain our young and attractive look, but we will grow old. The fashion and cosmetic industries make us feel young. Science and technology too. But the truth is that we are designed by nature to grow old.

Against this reality, it is important to ask yourself these questions: *What will ageing in marriage mean to me? How will I respond to the physical changes in my spouse?* Be honest with yourself. How will the changes influence your marriage? Spouses have walked out of their marriages because they no longer consider their spouses good-looking. This violates God's injunction. God says, particularly to men who are often guilty of this, *"Let her be as the loving hind and pleasant roe; let her breasts satisfy thee at all times; and be thou ravished always with her love"* (Proverbs 5:19). The phrases *"at all times"* and *"always"* mean perpetuity. You are meant to adore your spouse regardless of physical changes. Once you get married, you must stay married and be in a loving sexual relationship with your spouse. As you search for who to marry, hold this in your mind. It will help you avoid a partner that won't go the long haul with you.

6. Parenting

Another reality of marriage is your role as a parent. A husband is expected to be a father someday, just as the wife is expected to be a mother. As a father and grandfather, I admit that being a parent is not an easy job. Yet there is no happier role in life than raising great men and women. The joy of parents over the birth, growth, and success of their children is indescribable. The journey is not without toils and snares, but with God, you shall conquer.

Children have a great impact on marriage. They will place a huge demand on your time, emotions, finances, plan, space, etc. This means you will sacrifice yourself and your substance for your children. You will labour for them. You will give up some luxuries for the needs of your children. You will be expected to be disciplined, devoted, and loving parents. All of these and more are necessary because children must be brought up as godly seeds for the Lord. Children have a special place in the heart of God; they are His. "*Children are the heritage of the Lord, and the fruit of the womb a reward*" (Psalms 127:3). It is a blessing to be keepers of God's heritage.

The important questions are these: Will you be the kind of parent God desires? Will you go after someone that will be devoted to parenting? Will your partner make it a joyful and rewarding ride? Are you ready for the presence of children in marriage? These and many enquiries are crucial to your marriage. Several married and unmarried people today do not want children because of their high demand on marriage. You must, therefore, ascertain your role and your spouse's as parents.

7. Satanic Attacks

Satanic attacks on marriages are another dimension of marital realities. Unfortunately, it is rarely addressed prior to marriage. A lot of marriages are in deep-seated problems because of satanic manipulation. Some marriages have even collapsed.

In the preceding chapter, I enumerated six marriage assertions. Any of these truths is a sufficient reason for a satanic siege on marriage. The devil hates and wants to spoil anything that is meant to glorify God. The Bible tells us that *"The thief comes only to steal and kill and destroy" (John 10:10)*. Satan's cardinal objective is to destroy marriages. He will make an attempt to hijack your search for a suitable spouse. His scheme is to dominate your marriage and take over your home.

While you search for your spouse, you should be able to answer these questions: *Will I be able to stand against satanic attack on my marriage? Will my spouse join forces with me to protect our marriage? Will I have a spouse that can ward off advances of the enemy against our marriage? Will my spouse be able to stand before God to ensure that our home does not get trapped in the schemes of the enemy?* Your answers to these questions and many more should influence your choice of marriage partner.

Consequences

Many marriages have crashed today because couples are ignorant of the realities that await them. And many unmarried are not equipped spiritually because they are also ignorant of these realities. Consequently, they take wrong steps in marriage. They misinterpret marital crisis. And when marital issues prove too difficult for them to deal with, they become frustrated. Eventually, they lose grip of their marriages.

Behind every destroyed marriage, there is a

combination of human and spiritual inadequacies. Many homes cannot run smoothly because of unanticipated realities. Couples blame each other, fight, and go their separate ways. They become each other's enemy. They drag themselves through bitter and expensive litigations, which in reality make no one a winner. Soiled marital relationships, poor health, shame, ruined wealth, etc. are consequences of marriage realities that are inappropriately handled.

An adage says to be forewarned is to be forearmed. These realities of marriage are not meant to scare or discourage you. They should rather prepare you for marriage. Being aware, you will tread with caution before and after marriage. It will also make you acknowledge that you need the help of the Holy Spirit in marriage.

Although realities of marriage are destructive if mishandled, they can be easily controlled. Our assurance is founded on the Word of God which says: *"Little children, you are from God and have overcome them, for He who is in you is greater than he who is in the world"* (1 John 4:4 ESVi). With God by your side, you can overcome every negative reality against your marriage. Your eyes will be enlightened, and you will find the right marriage partner.

Guiding Light
Man in his pomp yet without understanding is like the beasts that perish.
(Psalm 49:20 ESVi)

> *The blessing of the LORD, it maketh rich,*
> *and he addeth no sorrow with it.*
>
> (Proverbs 10:22)

6
THE QUESTIONS YOU
MUST ASK

When wisdom entereth into thine heart, and
knowledge is pleasant unto thy soul; Discretion
shall preserve thee, understanding shall keep thee.
— Proverbs 2:10-11

Questions are healthy, particularly when a person seeks to understand a problem. They help us to focus on a subject that requires deep thoughts and valuable judgment. Marriage is a union that can make or break you. You must, therefore, understand it before you go into it.

Ask marriage-related questions from God and your mentors. This will help you along the way. Nothing is shameful in asking questions before you go into marriage. You should, by now, have tons of questions on some key areas covered in this book. Discuss them with God and mentors who are profound in spiritual matters.

Remember, successful people ask tons of questions every day. They use questions to: build on what they already know, know what they want to build, and know how to start building. They don't stop learning. The three reasons for asking questions are also relevant in marriage. You have enough reasons to seek answers from God and your mentors. So don't shy away from asking questions about where you are going and how to get there. Asking marriage-related questions produce answers that will enhance your understanding. These answers will assist you to make the right decisions. This is why this book encourages you to seek God's face in your search, and you must obey whatever He says.

God wants us to ask Him questions regarding our lives. He told Solomon, *"Ask what I shall give thee."* (See 1Kings 3:5) He is saying this to us today. Prophet Isaiah testifies to this truth when he said, *"Thus says the Lord, the Holy One of Israel, and his Maker, Ask of Me of things to come concerning my sons and concerning the work of My hands command ye Me"* (Isaiah 45:11). A believer must never be afraid of asking questions.

Marriage will have a significant impact on your life. It will influence your direction, aspirations, health, and wealth among others. Don't ignore the questions that come to your mind. Find answers. Satisfy your curiosity and observations. God and His chosen guides have answers that will empower and direct you towards a good marriage.

The Mother Of All Questions: Who should I marry?

A major question that should be on your lips right now is, "Who should I marry?" This question, from one of my sons, prompted this book. The question *"Who should I marry?"* is a bold enquiry. It is a pertinent question about marriage. And this is where your search for a spouse should start from. Answers will steer you in the right direction and prevent you from chasing after shadows. Answers will also save you from asking, *"Who have I married?"* in the future.

Nothing is better than being equipped with the picture of your spouse long before the search begins. Success is neither a result of impromptu action nor a product of wishful thinking. Success is anchored on divine direction and support. Asking the right questions will bring you into the zone of marital success.

Be Bold

Regardless of the benefits of questions, some people shy away from asking questions. In spite of the struggles in their heart, they won't ask questions. They won't ask questions that will give them insight into marriage. Oftentimes, people fail to ask questions due to these reasons:

1.   Self-conviction that there are no answers anywhere.
2.   Self-conviction that there are no creditable advisers.
3.   Weaknesses such as shyness, fear, pride, etc.
4.   Ignorance regarding the power of questions and answers.
5.   Spiritual deception and mind-games.

Don't allow these reasons to stop you from getting guidance on marriage. Failure to ask questions has consequences. It can end a promising relationship. It can also breed doubts, assumptions, etc. And love cannot blossom where communication is stifled.

The Bible says that *"Ye lust, and have not: ye kill, and desire to have, and cannot obtain: ye fight and war, yet ye have not, because ye ask not"* (James 4:2 KJV). We lack many things because of our failure to ask questions. You won't think or act right if you don't ask questions. I implore you to ask questions and find answers. Ask questions about how to find your Mr or Miss Right. You can also get answers by investing in similar books like this.

I have an adult son who asks questions concerning marriage. I have lost count of his whys, hows, whats, etc. about marriage. He discusses with his mum and me, knowing that we have his interest at heart. He is our son, and we want the best for him in life. As God has ordained and instructed us, we want to guide him into a successful marriage.

Our son is also engaged with his pastor and other spiritual mentors on the concerns of marriage. As a Christian parent, I am happy that my son seeks knowledge from the Holy Spirit. He also has trusted-people who will enlighten him on who, when, how, where to marry, and other important details.

I am happy to note that my son's questions are an expression of his earnest desire to have a successful marriage. From his testimony, he loves his happy family. He sees the endless love of God and love for God in my marriage. He wants the same and much more. He understands that premarital counselling helps his "how-to," and he does not shy away from it. He searches the Scripture for God's instructions on marriage; he asks the Holy Spirit to lead him. These are laudable steps expected from the unmarried. Your steps should be laudable as well.

A Warning To Consider

Matthew 7:7-8 says, *"Ask, and it will be given to you; seek, and you will find; knock, and it will be opened to you. For everyone who asks receives, and he who seeks finds, and to him who knocks it will be opened."* Here is a promise that all your questions or prayers will never go unanswered. Rest assured, you will find answers to your questions on marriage. And you will get understanding and find direction in marriage.

You must, however, be prepared to embrace these answers whether they are comfortable or not. Abide by every godly answer you receive. And ignoring godly answers is costly. If you won't obey God or His vessels, don't expect a successful marriage. Obey God, and you will not walk in error. He knows the end of your marriage from its beginning; so it is wise to submit to His leading. His answers might oppose your preconceived notions. However, remember that God does not operate on the level of your reasoning. He is far above the best of human intelligence. Hear what God tells us in John 15:5. *"I am the vine, you are the branches: He that abides in Me, and I in him, the same brings forth much fruit: for without Me you can do*

nothing." The success of your marriage rests on your
obedience to God.

Guiding Light

*Blessed is the man who remains steadfast
under trial, for when he has stood the test he
will receive the crown of life, which God has
promised to those who love him*

(James 1:12).

*"Submit yourselves therefore to God. Resist
the devil, and he will flee from you.*

(James 4:7).

7
STAY OFF MARITAL MISFITS!

Now we command you, brethren, in the name of our Lord Jesus Christ that ye withdraw yourselves from every brother that walketh disorderly, and not after the tradition which he received of us.
— 2 Thessalonians 3:6

Adhere to God's instructions regardless of your race, age, sex or status. Abiding in the Lord's directives creates highways to peace, joy, success, and prosperity. God promised us these things when He said: *"If you abide in Me, and My words abide in you, ask whatever you wish, and it will be done for you"* (John 15:7). We all want successful marriages and happy homes. These are the gifts of God to those who abide in His word. God has promised to grant us our desires in accordance with His will. We can have access to these gifts when we obey and allow Him to determine our marriage partner.

We obey God by avoiding those who are unfit for marriage — marital misfits. Life with marital misfits leads to sorrow and loss. Marital misfits are lethal weapons; you must protect yourself from them. Exchanging marital vows with a marital misfit is akin to making a pact with the devil. Beware! It is like entering into a lion's den. Such a den might seem calm and inviting. But make no mistake; a lion's den is deadly. Whoever enters an ominous relationship will be trapped and destroyed. Such a person will neither know peace nor happiness.

Marital Misfits

In this chapter, six groups of marital misfits will be examined. And you must avoid them as you search for a marriage partner.

Type One: THE UNBELIEVER

We live in a multicultural world. Wherever you go, you are bound to come across competing value systems, social beliefs, religious doctrines, traditions, and desires. The implication is that atheists, Satanists, occultists, idol worshippers, agnostics, Hindus, Muslims, and other non-Christians compete for your life and social participation. Each wants you as a convert, friend or spouse. The interesting thing is that they will be very polite and friendly. Their influence on you may be so soothing and hard to let go. But beyond their dispositions, they pledge their allegiance to spiritual powers that will oppose your Christian ethos.

You should know that everyone does not share your faith and values. Your Christian beliefs are detested by a lot of people out there. Atheists, for instance, maintain that the existence of God, Jesus Christ, and the Holy Spirit is a fable. To them, Christianity is fake. The Bible calls them fools. *"The fool says in his heart, 'There is no God.' They are corrupt, they do abominable deeds; there is none who does good"* (Psalm 14:1). The scripture here says: they are fools, corrupt, and they do horrible things. Don't marry someone whom God considers a fool. A corrupt person will ruin your marriage. Such a partner will pull you away from God. Many Christian women who got married to unbelievers have become victims of domestic violence because they attend church programmes or endorse Bible study sessions in their homes.

Do not marry anyone that has not accepted Jesus Christ as personal Lord and Saviour. Such a person is unfit for you. The evil voice that is set to ruin your future will challenge you. It will accuse you of prejudice; don't listen to it. But no campaign should make you ignore God's guiding principle for your life. If you willfully defy God's ordinance or spit on His authority, you will suffer grave consequences. You should always recall that anyone that denies God is a fool.

Marrying a believer paves the way for spiritual protection. *"Do not be unequally yoked with unbelievers. For what partnership has righteousness with lawlessness? Or what fellowship has light with darkness?"* (2 Corinthians 6:14) You carry the glory of God, and He calls you His light. It is your duty to protect the integrity of His ownership over you. And you can do this by not putting your redeemed life in an unholy marriage.

An unbeliever may satisfy your definition of a soft-spoken, pleasant, caring, and an intelligent person. Your choice of a partner might be handsome or beautiful. Such a person might please you well—to use the words of Samson to his parents when he fell in love with a woman who caused his destruction. Make no mistake; the devil has only come to kill, steal, and destroy. And he can act like an angel of light. Don't be deceived by the outward appearance of people. Don't be enchanted by the words of an unbeliever. If that person is not ready to surrender to God and accept Jesus Christ as Saviour, run! Heed the Lord's warning: don't marry an unbeliever.

There is another dimension to this issue which I must mention here. Every human being is a carrier of one form of spiritual entity or the other. Christians, for instance, carry the presence of the Holy Spirit. Non-Christians carry other spirit beings. Either way, the fact remains that the spirit in them will try to bring you under its dominion. This can mean utter destruction, poverty, and disgrace for your marriage. It may mean bouts of afflictions including sickness, childlessness, unemployment, untimely death, etc. Deuteronomy 7:26 cautions: *"And you shall not bring an abominable thing into your house and become devoted to destruction like it. You shall utterly detest and abhor it, for it is devoted to destruction."*

Stay away from unbelievers while searching for a marriage partner. A person that is not in Christ is volatile and vulnerable. Unbelievers are potential perpetrators and victims of various social ills. Due to their unbelief, unbroken ancestral ties, hexes, family afflictions, and evil covenants, they are susceptible to spiritual attacks. Their lives remain potential channels of devastating misfortunes, and anyone that goes into covenant with them will be scorched. Don't jeopardise your life and future. Withhold your wedding ring from anyone that says there is no God!

Misfit Type Two: BACKSLIDERS

A backslider is a person that deviates from Christian faith and principles, with no demonstrable attempt to return to the path of righteousness. The Bible says that such persons have made "*a shipwreck of their faith*" and have once again become entangled with worldly defilements. (See 2 Peter 2:20 and 1 Timothy 1:19.) Indeed, there are many unmarried and married people who derive pleasure in sin despite their awareness of God's ordinances. These set of people are liars, cheats, thieves, and manipulators. They are violent, greedy, and sneaky. Backsliders are unreliable and dangerous to live with. Flouting God's commandments can drive your marriage into the pit. Adultery, fraud, and other acts that destroy marriages are not far from backsliders.

Don't place your future in the hands of a deceitful person. Don't marry anyone who will dishonour you or your God. Many people are hurting today because of the actions and inactions of their spouses. Many have lost their minds and homes because their spouses are backslidden. If you don't want to join the statistics, avoid a backslider.

If backsliders can lie to government authorities, parents, spiritual mentors or friends, you won't be an exception. If you marry a hot-tempered and vicious partner, you might end up being a victim of domestic violence. A backslider can't keep marital vows.

The fear of God keeps us from committing sins. And by our commitment to God, we can stay safe. If you can't abide by what God says, you will hurt yourself and those around you. Similarly, you will hurt deeply if you marry a person with a backsliding tendency.

Don't allow a backslider to entice you into a journey of misery. You may be derailed from your goals and purpose if you marry one. Don't stake your life on a bad relationship. The Bible says, *"Do not be deceived 'Bad company ruins good morals' "* (1 Corinthians 15:33). You cannot live as a sinner in your marriage and expect the blessings of marriage. If an unrepentant backslider is unfit for the kingdom of God, such a person is unfit for holy matrimony.

Misfit Type Three: THE DESPICABLE

Watch out, certain members of this group may claim to be Christians. They may claim to know God. They attend church and read the Bible. But beware; they are as abominable as the two groups identified earlier. Their sexual orientation makes them despicable. Here is how the Bible describes them:

"For this reason, God gave them up to dishonourable passions. For their women exchanged natural relations for those that are contrary to nature; and the men likewise gave up natural relations with women and were consumed with passion for one another, men committing shameless acts with men and receiving in themselves the due penalty for their error" (Romans 1:26-27).

Note what the Bible says about them. They are men and women of perverted passions and strange sexual preferences. They no longer hold sexual affection or feelings that exist between married couples. Yet, sex remains a major element of a healthy and happy marriage. Sex is a medium ordained by God for human procreation. It is a medium of pleasure meant for a wife and her husband.

Sadly, this is a major area of attack in many homes. A lot of spouses suffer in silence from sexual abuse. The situation gets worse when either of the partners has a bizarre sexual need or orientation. Sodomy, homosexuality, bestiality, child-sex, wife-swinging, group sex, etc. have become rampant today. In Romans, we see same-sex copulation as a sin that has been in existence for a long time.

The message here is plain: know the sexual orientation of your choice of partner. Ask your partner sex-related questions. Weigh the answers against the backdrop of God's word. Watch out for clues and form your opinion about the sexual behaviour of your partner. Ask God to reveal hidden things about your partner. You may see questionable traits in your partner; probe further. Discuss your observations with your spiritual mentors.

If you are being pressured to have sex outside wedlock, run. The Bible encourages this line of action when it says, *"Flee from sexual immorality. Every other sin a person commits is outside the body, but the sexually immoral person sins against his own body"* (1 Corinthians 6:18). Flee the pressure and enticement to have sex outside of wedlock. Run away from anyone who tries to influence you to rebel against God. Tolerating such a person will make you sin against God, and it can break your marriage.

In the world of today, children suffer sexual abuse in the hands of parents with inordinate sexual behaviour. When a spouse engages in extra-marital affairs, it kills. But you will save yourself from disaster if you avoid a promiscuous marital partner.

There are many cases of couples who discovered that their spouses were sexually molesting their children, having sex with unknown persons, visiting prostitutes, gays, etc. Read their pathetic stories in the tabloids, and you will find lives torn into shreds. Promiscuity shatters marriages. It breeds damage, disease, stress, and untimely death. A young pregnant woman committed suicide by jumping down from a building when she found out that her husband had been sleeping with her mother. It was heart-wrenching for those who saw the video on social media.

More of such sad cases are kept away from the public glare, but with no less wounded hearts. A victim once told me that in the first month of her wedding, she caught her husband in bed with their best man. Unknown to her, she had married a gay whose best man was his bed-mate. Another woman mentioned that her husband convinced her to delay raising children, only to announce in the ninth year of their marriage that he was gay and really did not want children. She was distraught and almost lost her mind.

Apostle Paul wrote to the Church in Corinth: *"I wrote you in my letter not to associate with sexually immoral people* (1 Corinthians 5:9). This is still the code of conduct for every believer today. As a Christian, cross out from your list homosexuals, bi-sexual and others who engage in despicable sexual acts. Do not fall prey to sexual predators. The Bible does not permit sex outside of marriage. If you indulge in sex before marriage, you will ruin your chances of finding a partner that values your chastity. So don't be pressurised to engage in sex before marriage. If your partner cannot wait until marriage, keeping away from extra-marital affairs might be difficult for such a person.

Sex influences the direction of a marriage. It is sacred before God, and there are guidelines for it. But to a morally corrupt person, sex is not sacred. Such an individual sees sex as a mere expression of pleasure that can be satisfied anywhere, anytime, and with anyone. You are precious in the sight of God. You are too valuable to Him to be wasted on the altar of lust. Do not marry a sexually immoral spouse.

Misfit Type Four: THE IGNORAMUS

The word "ignoramus" is used here to describe those who are ignorant of the importance of marriage. Marriage covenant means nothing to them. Worst of all, they are not interested in finding out, yet they are interested in marriage. They simply love the idea of being married. And they are on the search for someone like you.

Anyone devoid of understanding about marriage can become vulnerable. Such a person will:

- Pursue short-term goals.
- Feel threatened at growth opportunities and challenges in marriage.
- Resist realities that should be appropriately received.
- Feel insecure by the vision, drive, and achievements of their spouses.
- Destroy anything and anyone in marriage while trying to figure things out.
- Quit instead of acquiring the knowledge of building a successful marriage.

Due to lack of wisdom and commitment to godly realities, the scribes and the Pharisees were called blind leaders who are set for the gutters. *"Let them alone. They are blind guides. And if the blind lead the blind, both will fall into a pit"* (Matthew 15:14). This admonition is apt for the kind of marital unfit mentioned here. You have to steer off every ignoramus if you are considering whom to marry.

Today, many married men and women exclaim:

"He (she) just doesn't care!" "Not ambitious!" "Never takes anything concerning this marriage serious!" "Just does not understand me!" "Never satisfied!" "My spouse does not respect me or take me seriously." "I can't sit with him (her) and plan for our future." "Nothing I do is ever pleasing to her (him)!" "Since I married, it has always been a struggle to move up in life!" "If only I had the support of my husband (wife)!" "I regret it! Saddled in a non-achieving marriage!" "My wife (husband) is not a goal-getter, just complacent with life!" Behind these sad expressions are victims of the ignoramus. They married people who know nothing about marriage. Don't be one of them.

The truth is, you might not easily notice an unserious person. Hence the need for you to watch out for the aspirations of whomever you want to marry. Know the person's thoughts on marriage. If you see signs of mediocrity, don't hesitate to leave that person. Marriage gives room for elevation. And you need someone you can work with, not someone that will pull you down. Ask God to help you discern the strengths and weaknesses of your prospective spouse and give you the wisdom to take appropriate action.

I'll conclude this segment with a note of caution: don't marry anyone who wants you as property. Don't marry anyone out of pity or emotions because it is difficult to change the ignoramus. Don't marry as a favour; you should rather marry out of mutual love and commitment to marital success.

Misfit Type Five: THE TOUCH NOTS

God forbids you to have sex with certain individuals in your life. These individuals may be Christians of attributes that make excellent partners. But you are forbidden from marrying them. Simply put, God has pronounced them unfit for you to marry.

The Bible reveals them in Leviticus 18:6-18 which states that *"No one shall approach any blood relative of his to uncover nakedness (have intimate relations). I am the LORD. You shall not uncover the [c]nakedness of your father... your mother... your father's wife... your sister... daughter of your father or of your mother... your son's daughter or your daughter's daughter... your father's wife's daughter... your father's sister... your mother's sister... your father's brother's wife... your daughter-in-law... your brother's wife... her son's daughter or her daughter's daughter... You shall not marry a woman in addition to her sister as a rival while she is alive, to uncover her nakedness."*

From the biblical excerpt, God warns us against incest — marriage or sexual relations between family members. Christians cannot marry any of their family members. Consequently, you must not marry the following persons:

1. Your brother or sister.
2. Your stepbrother or stepsister.

3. Your mother or your father
4. Your grand-father or grand-mother.
5. Your stepmother or stepfather.
6. Your cousin, nephew or nieces.
7. Your uncle or aunt.
8. Your uncle-in-law or aunt-in-law.

In today's world, people marry their first and second cousins. We have heard of brothers and sisters marrying each other. As at the time of writing this book, a young man and his mother in Zimbabwe were stopped by the court from marrying each other even though the mother was already pregnant for her son-turned-lover. This reveals the decadence in the marriage institution. Regardless of how appealing it is to "keep it within the family" as promoted by some tribes across the world, God calls it defilement. And it is condemnable by eternal death.

It also has an implication on the health of children. Medical reports show congenital diseases and disabilities suffered by children in marriages where their parents were siblings or close relations.

Don't join in the perpetuation of such abomination. Don't commit incest. It is utter disobedience to God. And the consequence is too great to imagine. *"Cursed be anyone who lies with his sister, whether the daughter of his father or the daughter of his mother." And all the people shall say, "Amen"* (Deuteronomy 27:22).

Misfit Type Six: THE RAVENOUS WOLVES

Some men and women are in search of people who will satisfy their lusts and inadequacies. They are predatory by nature. When it comes to making a good kill, predators are patient, focused, and brutal. Some of them put up disguises to escape being detected by their potential victims. They pretend to be who they are not. And I love to call them ravenous wolves.

These human wolves want you only for their selfish ends. What sustains them is what they can draw out of you in marriage. This may be sex, image, social status or money. Their goal centres on what they can get from you. Your marital expectations have no room in their hearts. If marrying you is a means of getting what they need, they will do it because they can exit your life anytime.

A female friend described this sad reality when she sent me the following words: "George (not real name) only wanted me for a visa. He married me so that he could become a British citizen. The moment he got it, I was cooked! He left me!"

George had left her and their three young children. He walked out of a seemingly happy ten-year-old marriage, straight into another woman's arm. To the amazement and disappointment of his relatives and friends, George walked out of his home. His ex-wife almost lost her mind over the incident. I guess anyone would have felt the same way too.

This kind of ugly incident has been on repeat in the world. We see spouses who break the hearts of their partners and children. They walk away from their homes, leaving mayhem behind. They will achieve their objectives at all cost, including plotting the death of their spouses.

For instance, the Mail Online reported on February 26, 2019, that a woman, Bdour Mohammed-Ali Al-Yasari (28), sent her lover, Jacob Joseph Ficher (27), to kill her husband, Ammar Al-Yasari, at his home in Holt, Michigan. As sad as this is, it's only one of the many murders in marriages.

In another devastating case, a mother of three teenagers left her husband and children. She moved into her friend's flat on the same street. Her friend was a middle-aged woman and single parent. Neighbours knew them to be very good friends until they found out, to their horror, that they were lovers. Both women admitted to their families and friends that they had been lovers for a while, and they decided to come out because they were tired of living a life of lies. Did this issue traumatise their relatives and friends? Yes, it did.

These kind of stories are not strange to many people today. And there will be uglier ones tomorrow. In this emerging era, "ravenous wolves" will be everywhere. Be on your guard, and stay away from them. See how 2 Timothy 3:2-3 puts it:

> *"This know also, that in the last days perilous times shall come. For men shall be lovers of their own selves, covetous, boasters, proud, blasphemers,*

disobedient to parents, unthankful, unholy,
Without natural affection, trucebreakers, false
accusers, incontinent, fierce, despisers of those that
are good, Traitors, heady, highminded, lovers of
pleasures more than lovers of God; Having a form
of godliness, but denying the power thereof: from
such turn away."

You will save yourself from a failed marriage if you turn away from predators. Back off from anyone that is set to plunder you. That's a command from God. Obey it. Don't marry someone who will use and dump you. Don't set yourself as a victim of exploitation; watch out for ravenous wolves.

When these wolves cannot get what they want in marriage, they will throw tantrums. Predators get frustrated easily, and when they do, they turn nasty. They unleash violence, verbal abuse, malice, anger, etc. on their spouses, children, relatives, and friends. No life is safe in the hands of a predator.

You can beat off every ravening wolf from your life. But this will require you to see through their disguise. To do this, you need God to help you. And through the power of the Holy Spirit, we can beat back evil advances against our lives. Make no mistake; you need the Spirit of God to protect you from the snares of the fowler.

Alertness And Obedience

Although I only identified six types of martial misfits

here, there are many more out there planning to make a mess of their captives. I pray that God will open your eyes to see them. They are set to hurt their partners; don't accept a marriage proposal from them.

A happy marriage is possible, but it won't be with a misfit. Therefore, be watchful as you search for a spouse. As emphasised in this book, you will succeed if you do these:

- Strictly obey God's word.
- Arm yourself with aspects of the Scripture on marriage.
- Read books on marriage by Christian authors.
- Take counsel from your spiritual mentors.
- Attend Christian marriage seminars.
- Pray without ceasing on the kind of marriage you seek.
- Discuss the kind of marriage you desire.
- Have a God-given image of your spouse.
- Know what you want and open your eyes wide!
- Go after the right person for you.

Yes, You Surely Can

An elderly woman once told me: "Kay, I know that what my daughter did was wrong—dating her best friend's ex-husband. But you see, you cannot help who you fall in love with." Wow! What nonsense! I felt a mother has just painted her daughter a wimp by endorsing such shameful behaviour. Adultery, fornication and other forms of sexual immorality are sins, and they destroy souls. *"He who commits adultery lacks sense; he who does it destroys himself"* (Proverbs 6:32 ESVi).

The old lady's assertion, *"you cannot help who you fall in love with"*, is a lie and an erroneous cliché which mocks the concept of love. You hold the power to determine who has your heart. God has given you that ability; you can do ALL things through Jesus Christ (See Philippians 4:13). You are a rational and spiritual being created by God. You have the power to control your needs, make good choices, and satisfy your wants. Surely, you can decide not to fall in love with a misfit.

You owe it to yourself to be happy in life. Your marriage should be an arena of peace and prosperity. The choices you make today are indispensable to your marriage. Therefore, do not accept a misfit as your spouse.

Guiding Light
See to it that no one takes you captive by philosophy and empty deceit, according to human tradition, according to the elemental spirits of the world, and not according to Christ
(Colossians 2:8 ESVi)

Be not wise in your own eyes; fear the LORD and turn away from evil
(Proverbs 3:7 ESVi).

8
THE SUITABLE SPOUSE

Charm is deceitful, and beauty is vain; But a woman who fears Yahweh, she shall be praised.
— Proverbs 31:30 WEB

From the preceding chapters, you were advised to take caution against marital destruction. Considering the physical and spiritual complexities of today's world, you can be saved by marrying a true child of God. In plain language, your ideal spouse must be godly. This chapter focuses on why a godly person is an ideal marriage partner. It also reveals how to identify a godly person.

Primary Attributes

The attributes of a godly person are many, but the essential ones are enumerated here.

A godly man or woman is a person that:

- has accepted Jesus Christ as personal Saviour.
- subscribes to the Lordship of Jesus Christ.
- subscribes to the leading of the Holy Spirit in all things.

- daily upholds God's word in thoughts and actions.
- goes after godly wisdom, knowledge, and understanding on issues of life.
- attends church services and programmes actively.
- believes in the tenets of Christian marriage.
- desires a happy Christian marriage.
- appreciates godly attributes and commitment to God in others.
- wants you as a spouse out of God-driven volition.
- respects your parents, family, socio-economic background and values.
- loves you unconditionally.

Before you decide to spend the rest of your life with someone, ensure that these attributes are found in that person. People may argue that there are non-Christian couples whose marriages are doing well. Yes, there are. Anything is possible with the grace of God. But there are countless marriages that, by reason of the ungodly attitude of the wife, husband, or both, have ended in tragedy. Some collapsed completely because they did not give God a chance in their home. The question is, *which path do you wish to follow*? Before you give an answer to this question, reflect on this admonition from the Book of Proverbs 27:12 which says, *"The prudent sees danger and hides himself, but the simple go on and suffer for it."*

Do not gamble with your life. Don't go into a relationship where your co-traveller neither knows God nor accepts Jesus Christ as Lord and Saviour. A godly person appreciates the divine purpose of marriage and knows God's interest in it. We can safely conclude that such a person will treat marriage as a sacred union and protect its sanctity. This is the kind of person you should marry.

When Tough Times Hit

Do you remember the realities of marriage discussed earlier in this book? The realities mean one thing: marriages are not without challenges. The challenges can be rough and stormy. But couples that follow God's leading will survive. When realities of marriage hit with aggression, those with the knowledge of God know what to do to keep sailing. Sadly, those without God often tremble, stumble, and fail. Because they don't know God, they take wrong turns into where tears and sorrow dwell. And they end up being separated or divorced.

There is no God like Jehovah. He alone makes the difference. You have every opportunity to get the right marriage partner. Look out for the godly attributes enumerated above and base your preference on them.

I presume that you want a happy marriage. And you want to see God glorified in your life. To make this a reality, you need a partner that also loves God. Marry a person that will celebrate you as a divine gift. Getting a godly spouse is not a fantasy. Don't ever assume that you can't get a perfect person. Because everything is possible with God, your heart's desire will be granted. Have faith in God while you diligently search the right stock for your spouse.

The right stock comprises the children of God. They carry God's DNA and possess His Spirit. And since you are a child of God, you should marry one. Remember that light has nothing in common with darkness. You have been forewarned in 2 Corinthians 6:14: *"Do not be yoked together with unbelievers. For what do righteousness and wickedness have in common? Or what fellowship can light have with darkness?"*

Badly-behaved Couples

In the last three decades, I have observed many marriages across the world. And a common feature of successful marriages is divine governance. The couples submit to God. They allow Him to reign in their lives and home. They plan their marriage with reverence to God. They know how to put their burdens before Him. And these spouses celebrate each other's presence.

On the other hand, collapsed marriages comprised couples who rejected God's intervention in their home. The couples concerned, or at least one of them, freely traded bitterness, lack of forgiveness, evil-speaking, hatred, greed, etc. in marriage. Some even gave themselves to sexual immorality. They refused God's touch. Hence, they rejected godly counsels and advice from those around them. They subjected themselves to demonic manipulations and crashed their marriages.

No one builds a marriage with a son or daughter of Belial without suffering regrets. Who is a child of Belial? The lawless, disobedient, unruly, idol worshipper, drunk, adulterer, liar, sexually immoral, and opposer of good. The list is endless. The hands of a child of Belial will suffocate any marriage to death.

The Bible advises us to avoid transactions with sons and daughters of Belial. *"Enter not into the path of the wicked, and go not in the way of evil men. Avoid it, pass not by it, turn from it, and pass away. For they sleep not, except they have done mischief; and their sleep is taken away, unless they cause some to fall"* (Proverbs 4:14-16). These words are for you. Enter not into their path. Stay away! Don't settle for a person that will treat you as thrash! The word of God again says, *"Do not give dogs what is holy, and do not throw your pearls before pigs, lest they trample them underfoot and turn to attack you"* (Matthew 7:6).

You are precious to God. So treat yourself with the dignity that you deserve. This starts by marrying a person that will cherish and treat you as God wants. Marry someone who will enhance your growth, honour your parents, and embrace your family—a person in whose hands you are safe!

Physical, Social and Material Attributes

We are often attracted to a person that we deem intelligent, smart, beautiful or handsome. We all do. Naturally, we want to find out more about the people we fancy. We, therefore, enquire about their:

- Family background
- Age
- Marital status
- Education
- Religion
- Nationality and ethnic background
- Career
- Work engagement
- Ambition
- Abode
- Lifestyle
- Achievements
- Friendships

Curiosity is healthy, but it is only profitable when it is right. It is normal to be curious about your potential marriage partner. Don't feel guilty for checking out the person's attributes. Make enquiries from people. Check the person out on Facebook, Instagram, LinkedIn, and other social media platforms. The Bible encourages us to know everything about those who ignite our interest. *"Beloved, do not believe every spirit, but test the spirits to see whether they are from God, for many false prophets have gone out into the world"* (1 John 4:1). Note the phrase "every spirit." This includes everyone. Investigate anyone you are interested in, using every available source of information. You will find useful information that will aid your decision.

But be warned: good looks, profession, wealth, family background, social connections, etc. are surface factors. They do not necessarily express the personality or moral and spiritual values of a person. And they do not guarantee a happy marriage. Look around; you will see that these factors can fail. Many handsome and rich men have lost their homes, just as many beautiful and wealthy women. There are professional but divorced workers in every community. Their social and personal attributes could not keep their homes. Divorce does not know wealth or poverty. It is not intimidated by beauty or ugliness. Separation has no respect for social connections, family background and many other things we consider valuable.

While you may feel attracted by these attributes in any person, understand that they are not the pillars upon which an enduring marriage is built. Look beyond these attributes. Without God, no other anchor can hold your marriage in times of storm. Thus, look out for godly attributes in your partner before marriage.

Desire Godly Attributes

Speaking of desiring godly attributes, my wife's testimony will serve as a good example. She has shared it many times to encourage people and express gratitude to God. She desired a man with the fear of God for a husband long before we met thirty-one years ago. She told me and many others that she would pray to God to make her marry His child. She asked God to grant her a husband that would be a strong believer, leading her and her children in the way of God. She desired a man with whom she would worship God always.

The exciting part is that Caroline's prayers took place many years before we met. More intriguing is the fact that I was far from being the kind of man in her prayers. I was not a Christian, and my fun-filled life was obviously far from being called pious, though I was not into crime, drugs or such things. Hence, when I met Caroline, as much as she liked me, she did not want me as a spouse. She was bold about it. It did not matter to her if I walked away. All that she wanted was a man whom God had chosen for her. Nothing I had was valuable to her as long as I was not a child of God. She told me, in plain terms, that all she ever wanted was a man with a heart for God, with whom she could worship God and who would bring up her children in the way of God. She was not going to settle for any man with no potential to fulfil her desires.

Somehow, I saw her spiritual conviction to raise her home for God. And I respected it. But strangely, I identified with it, and I loved her the more. I could not walk away even when I tried. I saw my life changing fast: the person she requested from God was emerging in me. When she accepted to marry me, she was convinced that God had answered her prayers by giving her a man of His choice. Thirty-one years after, we are still passionate about God. We have a Christian home and children that are fervent for the Lord. We could not have achieved these without God. We daily encourage each other in the word of God. We remain obedient to divine instructions regardless of the challenges. And Jesus Christ remains the Lord and Captain of our home.

The import of Caroline's testimony is that God answers prayers. He will grant you a godly spouse if you ask Him and follow the principles in this book. If any man or woman rejects your commitment to a Christian marriage, run! You have not found a suitable spouse. The Bible says, *"Do two walk together, unless they have agreed to meet?"* (Amos 3:3 ESVi) In your search, don't lose sight of this eternal truth. Don't marry anyone who opposes your spiritual principles. And don't deceive yourself that such a person will change after marriage. The power of salvation is not in your hands or in marriage. It is in the hands of God through Jesus Christ. If the person doesn't become a true believer before marriage, there is no guarantee that marriage will make such a person a believer.

Genuine Love Is Possible

At this stage, we can now talk about genuine love. Genuine love is an attribute of God, and it exists in godly people. It is one of the manifestations of the Holy Spirit. The best description of this kind of love is presented in Paul's letter to the Corinthians. It reads:

> *"Love is patient and kind; love does not envy or boast; it is not arrogant or rude. It does not insist on its own way; it is not irritable or resentful; it does not rejoice at wrongdoing, but rejoices with the truth. Love bears all things, believes all things,*

> *hopes all things, endures all things. Love never ends…"* 1 Corinthians 13:4-8

We all desire genuine love in marriage. You need a spouse who will encourage, support, and protect you – a spouse that will be patient with you, treat you with respect, and appreciate God in your life. You yearn for a spouse that will keep no record of wrongs but will allow love, peace, and joy to reign in your relationship – a spouse that intercedes on your behalf and creates an environment for your aspirations to flourish. These and many more are expressions of genuine love between godly couples. And the good news is that you can experience these in your marriage. Marriage is a fountain of God's blessing beyond the frontiers of man's expectations. Simply allow God to lead your marriage. The Bible assures us that "…*No good thing does He withhold from those who walk uprightly*" (Psalm 84:11). Genuine love is a gift from God, and it is available to anyone who walks with Him.

Don't believe the lies that true love does not exist. However, do not confuse it with lust. If you do, you will receive spurious attention. Many people have married, only to realise within days of their marriage that their spouses were not in love with them. In arranged marriages particularly, parents, relatives, friends, etc. often force two people together in the name of marriage. They will encourage them by saying, "Don't worry, you will love your spouse later." And *later* means in the marriage. But such advice is misleading, and it often does not bode well for the couples.

Don't be forced into a loveless marriage. If your partner does not demonstrate true love, don't marry him or her. Don't live in fear of not finding someone who will love you genuinely. Turn to God, and He will send a godly person your way.

Guiding Light

Every good gift and every perfect gift is from above, coming down from the Father of lights, with whom there is no variation or shadow due to change (James 1:17).

Anyone who does not love does not know God, because God is love (1John 4:8).

9
A STEP-BY-STEP JOURNEY

For we would not dare to classify or compare ourselves with some of those who recommend themselves. But when they measure themselves by themselves and compare themselves with themselves, they are without understanding.
— 2 Corinthians 10:12

Marriage is a journey; it requires you to go out to find the right person for you. Failure and unfruitful efforts are not allowed. Non-starters and quitters don't know the taste of success. You should be active in your search for whom to marry. As a woman interested in marriage, go out there and search for him. Same for you if you are a man with an intention to get married. Successful people pursue what they desire passionately. Marriage is not an exception. Regardless of your sex, get up and work on your desire. Be determined to get the right person, and commit your determination into God's hands.

Start the journey today if you haven't started. From eighteen years upwards, you can commence this journey.

Seek the face of God on who to marry. The older you are, the more the need to prepare for marriage. The idea is for you to be focused on getting your marriage right.

A 51-year-old woman once said to me that she knew who her husband would be when she was only sixteen years old. And she was right. She married him, and they are still happily married to each other for over three decades. It was so delightful to see a woman who, in her teenage years, knew where she was going and what she wanted.

As typical of every successful endeavour in life, four things will be required of you on this journey:

1.   Good preparation
2.   Commitment
3.   Positive mindset
4.   Spiritual guidance

   Without these elements, your search will be weak and poorly coordinated. It will either lead you astray or to a dead end. Time and emotions will also be wasted. But proper preparation, commitment, positive mindset and spiritual guidance will prevent these negative outcomes.

Poor Search

A poorly-executed search produces a wrong marriage. It brings incompatible and ill-prepared persons together, labelling them as couples. Check around: you will find a host of unhappy and under-performing marriages.

Oftentimes, these are outcomes of badly-coordinated searches.

Today, several people are heart-broken because of failed relationships. When partners in a promising relationship take wrong steps, problems occur. And they end up hurting themselves and others. In some cases, a wave of uncertainty, argument, hatred, and issues that are capable of destroying healthy relationships will set in. The idea of marriage is unattractive to an aggrieved person. When one of the partners concludes that the relationship is not working, the partner will go out through the door.

Mr or Miss "Runaway" in an unsure journey often commands my sympathy. Unsure partners often doubt if another trial is worthy. They do not date. And when they do, they date wrongly, and end up repeating a poor performance. This should not happen to you. Walk away from a relationship that is not right, and use the experience to conduct better one.

Any would-be spouse in an unhappy relationship should quit as early as possible. Politely end a relationship that does not give you a hope of a happy marriage or future. *"A prudent person foresees danger and takes precautions. The simpleton goes blindly on and suffers the consequences"* Proverbs 22:3 NLT. A simpleton is a foolish person that ignores all the danger signs on a journey. Simpletons ignore future problems picked up by their spiritual radar, and they continue to walk towards marriage. You were not created to be a foolish person and you should not act as one. If a relationship is not working for you, end it.

Premarital breakups are often hurtful and difficult. The partners may feel used and dumped. They may feel that their emotion, time, and opportunity have been wasted. This feeling often leads to sorrow, fear, and low self-esteem. Sometimes, hatred, violence or suicide may arise. None of these reactions is from God. They are evil manifestations set to destroy anything and anyone in sight. To avoid a failed relationship, take appropriate steps from the starting point of your search.

God requires His children to do things decently. (See 1 Corinthians 14:40) Your journey into marriage must be conducted in an appropriate manner. As a child of God, you must follow divine directives. When you do, you will be saved from experiencing or inflicting pain. You will tread on the right path and escape relationship mishaps. You will also end up with the right spouse if you allow God to lead you.

Beware of Spiritual Thorns on your Journey

You will encounter some lies on your journey to marriage. Lies do show up in the journey of life for a purpose: to afflict us with fear, confusion, discouragement, hopelessness, and desperation. Each of these emotions will try to ruin your journey. But beware: lies are toxic spiritual thorns. They destroy their captives. If allowed, they will abort a search. Do not give in to lies. Do not be ignorant of your place in life. Ignorance will make you vulnerable. If you allow lies to overwhelm you, particularly in matters of marriage, your determination to conduct a successful search will fail.

Satan does not want you to succeed. He will try to stop you from entering a good marriage. He hates marriages and campaigns against it. This is not a surprise. Jesus told us that the devil comes to steal, kill, and destroy. Satan has a lot of human converts too; they will try to drive you away from marriage or lure you into a bad one. Therefore, you must always be on the alert. Getting the right spouse should be one of your most important decisions in life. And once you commit to this goal, the devil will try to ruin it. He will attempt to hijack every stage of your search for a suitable spouse. Do not give in. Don't allow him to frustrate your effort.

Step out with confidence. Know what you want in marriage, and be firm about it. Make godly decisions throughout your search. Trust in God, and work with Him until you get your spouse.

Common Lies

As mentioned above, through ignorance, many unwed hold on to lies. And this has changed their concept of marriage. Some people know this and will admit it. Sadly, many others do not know. Some of the lies are as follows:

- There is no perfect wife or husband.
- I can never get the perfect person to marry.

- I cannot get any other person that is more beautiful.
- There is no other person for me to marry.
- I can't get anyone that I like.
- I can marry anyone I want.
- No man or woman can meet my standards.
- The good wives or husbands have been taken.
- I am not good enough to marry.
- I do not have the call or patience to be a wife or husband.
- I am never going to be ready for marriage.
- I just want a child or children, not ready to tie myself down.
- Marriage is not really for me.
- Nobody wants me.

These are thorns on the path of marriage. Any of these can delay or stop your search. These lies can keep you from experiencing a happy marriage. These claims may appear reasonable, they are not. They are self-defeating claims. Any confession on your lips which does not align with the purpose of God for your life is evil.

Those who uphold any of these lies have the wrong concept of God and marriage. Except they change their mindset, they will disappoint anyone that marries them. Anyone who upholds these beliefs must be avoided.

God wants us to be honest and selfless. He detests the proud. His Word advises that we should not think more highly of ourselves than we ought to. (See Romans 12:3) This calls us to put on the garment of humility. If you are genuinely interested in marriage, rest in the fact that God has prepared the right spouse for you. Do not allow any lie to cheat you out of this divine provision.

Your spouse might be closer to you than you know. But you must make the right move. That move could be a change in your thoughts about marriage. It may be about breaking the yoke of defeating convictions that might stop you from pursuing what you want. Why will you dread searching for your spouse? Why will you assume that marriage is unworthy? Why will you nurse the idea that your marriage will end up in failure?

Proverbs 4:23 advises us: *"Keep your heart with all vigilance, for from it flow the springs of life."* I feel compelled to advise you thus: do not allow spiritual bandits to operate on your path. Break every chain of limitations and pursue your dreams. Don't allow anyone to rob you of your confidence. Trust in God as you embark on your marital journey.

Guiding Truth

For Whoever desires to love life and see good days, let him keep his tongue from evil and his lips from speaking deceit

(1 Peter 3:10).

> *Therefore, as you received Christ Jesus*
> *the Lord, so walk in him, rooted and*
> *built up in him and established in the*
> *faith, just as you were taught,*
> *abounding in thanksgiving*
> (Colossians 2:6).

10
The Most Essential Steps

Your word is a lamp to guide my feet and a light for my path. —Psalm 119:105

There are seven steps for a healthy search. The steps are in sequential order, and you should follow them according to the order they come up in this book. Doing so will enable you to conduct a coordinated search. It will also promote your chances of success.

Do not muddle things for yourself or anyone. The more you pay attention to each step of the search, the better the outcome. The book of 1 Corinthians 14:40 ESVi says, *"But all things should be done decently and in order."* Note the words, *all things*. You must take appropriate steps as and when due.

Walking in a decent manner includes paying attention to every step you take. But a lot of people are too impatient. They rush to the altar and rush out almost immediately. And those who hang on after rushing in, hang on in pain and disappointment. As they consider the way out, they wonder about where they went wrong. We should learn from these sad cases. Don't be in a rush to take steps that will cause you trauma in the future.

Each step of your search requires thorough examination and understanding. Observe what you see, hear or feel as you take each step. See how Ephesians 5:15-17 puts it: *"Look carefully then how you walk, not as unwise but as wise, making the best use of the time, because the days are evil. Therefore, do not be foolish, but understand what the will of the Lord is."*

Duration of the Search

What is the time span of searching for a spouse? To be candid, there is no one-time-fits-all. And my intention is not to recommend one, owning to the fact that what works for me might not work for you. The events that occur in our lives vary. God can choose to work with anyone in a unique timing. Therefore, the duration of your search may be different from someone else's search.

On the other hand, the steps suggested in this book can take place within three years. If you need more time to go through the steps, do so. Don't yield to inner or external pressure to rush into marriage. Remember, this is all about you and your future.

Every journey of life requires us to be on the alert and be patient. *"The thoughts of the diligent tend only to plenteousness; but of every one that is hasty only to want"* (Proverbs 21:5). To get the best out of the steps enumerated below, invest quality time and effort. Getting a good spouse is not a microwave affair. And marrying someone you barely know is dangerous.

Step One: THE CONTACT

This is the first step to take. It involves establishing contact with your potential spouse. Establishing contact is quite easy, but many people do not seem to share this confidence. They think that meeting a potential spouse is difficult. Some even convince themselves that they are not capable of finding their perfect match. Don't believe this because you will hurt your feelings. It can force you to lash out at anyone that comes close to you.

Many unmarried people have already made the first contact. But they do not know. This is true of individuals who eventually marry their colleagues, former classmates, next-door neighbours, church members, family friends, clients, etc. If you are searching for a spouse, start from the people that surround you. The person who is meant for you might be in your existing social circle. Two happily married and successful gospel ministers, on their 30th wedding anniversary, told their guests that they met each other in a church choir. Their first point of contact (FPC) was the choir.

Other people's *FPC* could be on the bus, plane, train or tube. It could be at a holiday resort, conference or workshop, family party, restaurant or church service. The FPC could also be on social media. The list is endless. These are ordinary places and events where people meet one another daily. They are rich grounds to start healthy relationships. So utilise your everyday interactions because they are filled with potential spouses.

You have tremendous opportunities to meet your

prospective spouse. Sometimes ago, a single young man got a job in a textile industry. Not far from his new workplace was a residential property where a pretty young girl lived with her elder sister. It did not take long for these two to notice each other and become good friends. They got married a few years later and remained happily married to each other for fifty years until the man went to be with the Lord. Their marriage was blessed with many riches including children, grandchildren, and great-grandchildren. How do I know this story? These two people gave birth to me. And my mum told me the story.

I have also told my children how I met their mum. I will share it with you shortly. And if you don't know how your parents met, ask them. Most parents tell their children similar stories. You may even know of so many others. You will note that it isn't complicated. And that you can do the same or better.

It is easy to meet your potential spouse. You might be even closer than you think because meeting people is an integral part of our daily lives. Simply allow God to direct your steps. Psalm 37:23 declares, "*The steps of a good man are ordered by the Lord: and he delighteth in his way.*" Commit your day to God, and He will direct your footsteps. When you turn to Him in honest submission, three things will happen:

1. God will draw you to godly people.
2. He will turn the hearts of godly people towards you.
3. He will enable you to maintain godly relationships.

Godly people are pleasant resources; they are a fountain of blessing. And your marriage partner should emerge from this bunch. You can marry a godly person. You probably have met that person who could be among the people you relate with, or someone you recently sighted. I had a personal experience of this.

Thirty-one years ago, I walked into the library of Social Science faculty at the University of Ibadan, Nigeria. I saw a young lady, waiting at the librarian's desk to be attended to. As I came through the door, we made eye contact. I smiled and must have mumbled a "hi" as I walked past her. She looked away. And I could not tell if she had returned my greetings. Hiding behind bookshelves, I stole a glance at her. She looked elegant and peaceful. I concluded that she was good looking, and I was attracted to her instantly. I watched her as she finished her business and exited the library. Did I go after her to chat her up? No. I felt that I should, but I didn't have the courage.

But God favoured me with a second chance just about a week later. I was at the post room of the Postgraduate Hall of Residence, checking for my letters. Suddenly I felt someone had queued behind me, waiting to check through the posts too. I turned around, and who did I see? The same lady I had seen at the faculty library. Again, I smiled and said "Hi". Posts delivered to the postgraduate students' hall of residence were filed in alphabetical order using the students' surnames. Seeing her behind me, waiting for the bunch of posts in my hand, I knew that our surnames must have the same initial letter K. I asked for her name, politely offering to check for hers too as I searched through the pile for mine. Without hesitation and with a shadow of a smile on her face, she offered me her full name. She was casually dressed, with no makeup, yet she looked more beautiful than the first time I saw her.

We had no posts. So we had to leave the post room. But I was smitten by this girl I barely knew. It was the proverbial *love-at-first-sight* experience for me. I walked her back to her room with excitement, chatting and joking as we climbed the stairs. At her doorstep, I asked if I could pop in sometimes. Without hesitation, she said "Yes." I pointed out the floor to my room and gave her the number. I added that she could pop in if she wanted to chat or needed a quieter room to study.

At this stage, a good friend of mine, who had witnessed all of these, pushed me aside and warned this girl to stay off my radar. We all laughed at his seemingly kind gesture to save a soft-spoken beauty from a Casanova. But my lovely friend, Ademola Adegbile, had no cause to worry. He saw the birth of a wonderful courtship that became a happy marriage three years later.

As you search for your spouse, watch where you go. Enjoy your first point of contact with people. Don't be nasty with those you're meeting for the first time. People are naturally drawn to well-mannered people. Don't stand aloof or look down on anyone. Be sensitive to those around you. When you feel drawn to a stranger, exchange pleasantries. Assess the situation, and if you feel safe and the occasion seems right, swap contact details too. That could be the beginning of your marital journey.

To step into this stage of your marital process, don't keep yourself locked up. Go out there and socialise. A friend's daughter, aged 31, told me that she had no boyfriend but would like to get married. Interestingly, she blamed her situation on the fact that she does not go out or keep friends. The father confirmed that she was a recluse. If you fail to explore your social circle and make friends, your opportunities to meet a potential spouse will be reduced. The Indian poet, Rabindranath Tago (1861 -1941) said, *"You can't cross the sea merely by standing and staring at the water."* I advised my friend's daughter to change her ways if she was interested in finding her potential spouse.

Connect with the right people. Interact with your colleagues. Get involved in church activities; visit places of interests; go on holidays. Be friendly to the people around you. You can't afford to be a recluse. Get spiritual and professional help if you are scared of meeting new people. People don't gravitate towards unfriendly people. Show interest in people, and they will show interest in you. Saying "Hello" to strangers will open new doors of opportunities for you. Don't hide behind the curtains and watch the world go by.

Not Yet! Just a seed!

At this stage of your search, your interest is to meet new people, particularly members of the opposite sex. Keep the idea of finding a marriage partner far from your mind. Someone you have just met is still a stranger, not a friend. Many people miss this point, and they end up doing abominable things such as having sex with total strangers and defiling themselves. Don't do anything that will bring you into utter condemnation.

Your initial contact is a seed. Like other seeds, it must be planted. It needs time to germinate, grow, and bear fruits. So, spend quality time to know a stranger well. Don't be in a rush. And don't throw yourself into the arms of a stranger. Don't be manipulated by fear or convince yourself that you need to move fast on your "catch." A lot of such fast moves have ended in ghastly accidents.

We are advised in Colossians 4:5 to *"Walk in wisdom toward outsiders, making the best use of the time."* Observe the stranger's words and actions because people are known by their words and actions. The words that you hear and do not hear; the habits that you see or do not see in the stranger will guide you. Bear in mind that at this stage, a Mr or Miss Stranger will most likely demonstrate pleasant behaviour. This underscores the indispensable place of the Holy Spirit in revealing the hidden things that can cause joy or sadness.

Ask God to show you hidden things about the stranger that interests you. And God will show you things beyond what your human eyes can see. *"Call to Me and I will answer you, and will tell you great and hidden things that you have not known"* (Jeremiah 33:3 ESV). This is a divine promise. God is ready to direct your steps and eliminate unhealthy relationships. Don't be weary of praying at any time in your search, particularly when you come across a stranger. And don't let down your guard with strangers.

Step Two: FORMING

A good friendship takes time to form. For a lot of happily married couples today, their transition from knowing each other to becoming great friends took months and years. This suggests that transition from being a stranger to a good friend is a function of time, but much more, it is a function of mutually satisfying interaction. This depends on the attributes you have both found and liked in each other.

What are the factors that facilitate friendship between two godly people? What are the qualities that will endear you to your prospective spouse? Whoever you want to make a friend must be:

- God-fearing.
- Trustworthy and honest.
- Loyal and committed.
- Caring and supportive.
- Able to trust others.
- Sympathetic and empathetic.
- Respectful and polite.
- A non-judgmental listener.
- Self-motivating and encouraging.
- Hard working and ambitious.

These ten qualities are sufficient to forge a friendship with a "stranger" that you have known for a while. The Bible advises us that bad company corrupts good manners (See 2 Corinthians 15:33) and as righteous people, we must choose our friends wisely (Proverbs 12:26). These admonitions provide your first pre-marriage target: don't associate with the wrong people. The kind of people you associate with will influence who you marry. You have no business with dishonest people other than preaching God to them. The Bible says that a dishonest man spreads strife, and a whisperer separates close friends. A dishonest and disrespectful spouse will hurt you. In the same vein, anyone that relishes sin should not be your spouse. Remember the word of God: *"Make no friendship with an angry man, and with a furious man do not go, lest you learn his ways and set a snare for your soul"* (Proverbs 22:24–25 NKJV).

As possible as you can, know everything about your potential friend. Know vital details such as family history and structure, educational background, religious affiliation, sexual orientation, hobbies, phobias, health issues, criminal records, etc. These are common information shared between friends. And the growth of every friendship depends on them.

Step Three: PRE-COURTSHIP
This is the stage where friendship starts having a tint of mutual interest. You and your friend will begin to enjoy

each other's company as you spend time together. If this feeling becomes a natural progression of your friendship, the relationship will be platonic. In other words, you will only be good friends with respect for each other.

At this stage, you are not *"having an affair."* This is the general description often used to express all manners of lustful relationships. This stage is for building the friendship. It is also for learning about your likes, dislikes, phobias, weaknesses, strengths, beliefs, knowledge, temperaments, talents, preferences, ambitions, visions, etc. During this stage, uncover your friend's personality. Be yourself, and let your true self be revealed so that you won't be misjudged.

Finding your spouse is a two-way street. While you are assessing your friend to know if you can proceed together, your friend is also doing the same. So be honest with each other. Don't pretend. I have come across people who hide their faith from those they are interested in. As Christians, the society wants us to hide our identity. But your faith is meant to shield you from misfits. It allows you to see a wolf that may come to you in a sheep's skin. As darkness and light cannot relate, so does an unrighteous person cannot stand with a righteous person. (See Psalm 1)

At the pre-courtship stage, ask questions about your friend. Ask questions to know:
- your friend's marital goals
- when your friend intends to marry
- the kind of person that your friend wants to marry·

- if your friend has been married before
- if your friend has sexual experience
- if your friend is in a relationship
- your friend's outlook on family setting
- your friend's perspective on family structure
- your friend's racial and family background
- your friend's spiritual beliefs

Don't make assumptions about your friend's past, present, and future. Assumptions can make a fool of you. Build your decisions on knowledge. Know the person you want to spend the rest of your life with. Keep checking, and be watchful. Search social media platforms. Check out your friend's posts. You may uncover expressions, viewpoints, and pictures that may halt your decisions. Compare and contrast your findings alongside your convictions. Compare your findings with God's word. Doing these will guide your decisions.

This is a complex situation, but you must continue until you've ascertained the future of your relationship. Be warned, however, because as you uncover comfortable things, you will also uncover uncomfortable things. Your discoveries should be taken to God in prayers. You can also discuss your findings with parents, pastors, spiritual mentors, etc. You will gain insight through their responses. And the answers will influence your direction—either to proceed to the courtship stage or terminate the relationships.

I will add an important message at this juncture. The Bible reveals in 2 Corinthians 5:17 that *"Therefore, if anyone is in Christ, he is a new creation; old things have passed away; behold, all things have become new."* This verse has always freed me from the grip of my past. It should also encourage you to desist from self-condemnation occasioned by your past. And by extension, do not judge believers by their forgiven past. Do not reject a believer on the account of the past. If you do, you may be throwing away a promising relationships.

We all have our pasts which contain ugly occurrences, particularly the rotten places we visited and the unholy things we did in the days of our ignorance. We all have a past that is stained by immorality, violence, wickedness, intolerance, impatience, etc. But with the blood of Jesus Christ, we are cleansed and renewed. We are no longer slaves to the past. Therefore, don't be held hostage by your past. And don't hold anyone hostage too. If you cannot accept a believer's past, you are not worthy of the believer's future.

Again at this stage of your search, do not engage in sex, kissing or any other form of sexual acts. Sex outside marriage is a sin before God. Do not allow God to abandon you in your "selection process." Keep your chastity intact regardless of the popular trend. Your life is the most precious asset you have. So honour God with it. Guide your life jealously by abstaining from sexual sins. You might be tempted to engage in premarital sex during this stage; you must not give in to temptation. Premarital sex will mess up your mind and spirit. And your sense of objectivity, which is essential for sound judgement, will be impaired. Worst of all, you might lose God's leading.

Step Four: COURTSHIP

At this stage, you and your friend know, without a shadow of a doubt, that you have a strong affection for each other. You are convinced that you are in love with each other. However, if you are uncertain about this, don't terminate the pre-courtship stage. Stay in pre-courtship stage and work things out. Re-evaluate your position. Don't take a step further if you are not certain of where you are heading. You might hurt each other's feelings if you proceed into courtship without preparation.

This stage also calls for spiritual discernment. You are closer to making a decision that can make or break you. A decision that will influence your life and affect your generations to come. So you need God's guidance. Proverbs 3:5-7 tells us to *"Trust in the Lord with all thine heart; and lean not unto thine own understanding. In all thy ways acknowledge him, and he shall direct thy paths."* Allow God to lead you, and you won't make a wrong decision.

Furthermore, you and your partner will start spending more time together. A lot of hidden habits will continue to unfold. An adage says that "Actions speak louder than words." Be sensitive. Consider all that you hear, see or feel about the other person in light of God's word and the future you anticipate. If you find some unacceptable signals, speak out. Discuss what you perceive. Observe the feedback you get. This should reveal how both of you will deal with issues in your marriage.

Money and communication have a great influence on marriage. They either promote mutual love, care, and respect or attract argument, hostility and hatred. It all depends on the attitude of either partner. During courtship, know your partner's spending habit, financial goals, beliefs about money, etc. You don't want to marry someone who will be a negative force in building and managing wealth. We have identified the ravenous wolves among marital misfits. Avoid them. Likewise, a miser, gambler or spendthrift will ruin your chances of building wealth.

On the subject of communication, observe how your partner speaks to you and others. And appreciate how your partner wants to be spoken to. Note the body language of your partner. You will speak and listen to each other for a very long time if you get married. For this reason, you must have a healthy conversation. Be certain that your conversations won't become poisonous jibes in the future. Communication between two people, who are right for each other, should be peaceful, comforting, and motivating. And their communication won't be affected by challenges.

The courtship stage is also the appropriate time to consider if your aspirations align. Your aspirations don't have to be exactly the same, but they should not oppose each other. Your aspirations should be complementary. Talk about your desires and convictions on children, family size, financial plans, preferred location of residence, career growth, etc. In all of these, ask questions to determine if both of you are compatible for marriage.

At this stage of your journey, you should be able to perceive if your friend is the Mr or Miss Right. But bear in mind that being good friends with someone does not mean you are suitable as marriage partners. Courtship often clarifies this.

Step Five: FORMAL PRESENTATION

This is the stage where you are convinced that you have found your Mr or Miss Right. It is an extension of the courtship stage, where you and your partner formally interact with each other's relatives and associates. During this stage, you will introduce your potential spouse to your:

- Parents
- Pastors
- Spiritual mentors and/or guardians
- Siblings
- Family members such as grandparents, uncles, aunts, etc.
- Friends

Your partner will also accord you the same courtesy. So be prepared to be invited to visit your partner's parents. You will also attend church services, social events, family birthday parties, marriage ceremonies, etc. with your partner. Formal introduction to each other's parents and family members is important.

Meeting the people in the life of your potential spouse should not be passive. It must be planned and properly executed. Both of you have the duty of facilitating this stage. Allow your partner to take the lead, and take the lead as well when it is your turn. Don't forcefully demand to meet your partner's family members or friends. You both have the right to determine when it is appropriate to present each other to the people that matter in your lives.

Your individual and mutual direction show:

- how well you are desired and at what pace.
- any hesitation in your potential spouse that must be addressed.

This stage of your relationship does not have to be rushed through. You both know your family members well. And you know when and how to approach them. "Bringing home" a boyfriend or girlfriend varies according to culture, family ethics, structure, and beliefs. Summarily, if it is an easy task with your family, it might be difficult with your partner's family. In my own case, my parents were always happy to see their children's friends at our home in Lagos, a cosmopolitan city in Nigeria. My street had no gated building, but multi-residential houses where children and adults play with one another and chat all day long. My parents had their doors wide open to all. In that setting, our house was always filled with people, many of whom were male and female friends, dating back to our primary, secondary, and university days. My parents knew almost all the boys and girls that visited us. When I was ready to formally introduce my spouse, I didn't struggle. Caroline had been a regular visitor to our house. And my parents liked her. When they knew she was the one I wanted to marry, they were excited. I received no comment or gesture from them or my siblings that suggested a reservation against my choice. They were all happy for me, and they showed it.

My experience was a bit different from that of some of my friends. I had male and female friends who could not receive friends in their homes. Their homes were "no-go" areas. The ban was in place even when they had grown into young adults, including university graduates. Many of them struggled to introduce their fiancés or fiancées to their parents.

You should respect the feelings and reservations of your partner about introducing you to relatives. However, don't be passive about this. Fear might not be the only reason for your partner's reluctance, factors such as shyness, anxiety, procrastination, etc. might also trigger it. If you see any of these in your partner, don't panic or take offence. Discuss with your partner. And get to see how you can both move past this point. Discussing this with your partner presumes that you will have some questions on your mind such as: "Why is my partner delaying to introduce me to the family members?" "Does this person have doubts about me?" "Does my partner know how the parents will react when they meet me?"

Endless questions and thoughts will visit your mind. These questions are healthy, and you must not allow them to turn into fear, anger or frustration. Work on every hurdle, and help your partner to resolve the hurdle.

Considering the fact that you know how best to approach your family, do not dictate when you must meet your partner's family. Don't appear desperate. Don't throw a tantrum either. It could damage your credibility. You should rather be empathetic.

If you notice an ominous delay in your relationship, seek a solution. Make an effort to know the source of the delay. Work with your spouse, and take the situation to God in prayers. Get your loved ones to pray with you. Discuss with your mentors; let them know about the delay. Take counsel from them because *"Without counsel plans fail, but with many advisers they succeed"* (Proverbs 15:22). On a general note, it is normal for people to get cold feet during their journey to marriage. If you experience such, identify the trigger — physical or spiritual — and deal with it.

The Big Caution
Don't be kept waiting unnecessarily, particularly during courtship. A lot of people are time-wasters. They are demonic agents sent to delay or derail your journey. Don't allow them to waste your time. Time-wasters who profess love are dangerous. They are also elusive, and a love-stricken partner might not spot them easily. You need the

Holy Spirit's help to discern them and flee their grip before it is too late. God will shield you from anyone that wants to put your life on hold. He will show you the way out. But there is a demand on your part: allow God to lead you. Do not search for your spouse without God. Walk with God and follow His dictates.

As children of God, delay should not discourage us because no form of delay can defy God's power. So don't be anxious when you experience a delay in your life. With God by your side, every delay against your progress shall come to an end. It does not matter if the delay is in getting a job or promotion, starting a business, buying a house, or finding the right person to marry. As long as you trust in God, every delay will retreat.

Get Feedback

You must get feedback from those you introduce your potential spouse to. A lot of people fail to do this because they don't know its importance. Courtship is the stage where your relationship is accountable to the people you hold in high esteem. These include your parents, siblings, pastors, and mentors. Introducing your partner to them is, in its essence, a mere presentation. And presentation invites responses. Therefore, be available for comments, questions, and suggestions from your loved ones.

Don't forget that even in courtship, you are still considering if your partner is the right person for marriage. Thus, after introducing your partner, get feedback. Every concern raised by your loved ones is significant. Take their thoughts into consideration, and don't dismiss their suggestions. Your loved ones have the right to evaluate your steps and advise you on who you have "brought home."

Their remarks will come to you at different points. If you do not get any, ask them. There is no harm in asking your parents, siblings, aunts, uncles, friends, etc. about what they feel about your partner. Remember what I said earlier in this book: when it comes to searching for a marriageable partner, you need your parents and spiritual guardians. God placed them in your life for a reason. So make it a priority to know their thoughts.

God expects your parents to guide you on the right path of life. About Abraham, he said: *"For I know him, that he will command his children and his household after him, and they shall keep the way of the Lord to do justice and judgment, that the Lord may bring upon Abraham that which He hath spoken of him"* (Genesis 18:19). Every God-fearing parent will like to follow Abraham's steps and earn the same testimonial from God. Genuine Christian parents urge their children to follow God's commandments. Your parents, particularly Bible-believing parents, want you to succeed. Therefore, do not begrudge your parents or loved ones when they raise concerns about the person you introduce to them. Listen, learn, and act appropriately. Your marriage is one of your parents' responsibilities towards you. And they fulfil this duty by offering godly counsels.

Another major feedback you will get by introducing your partner to your loved ones is your partner's reaction to your loved ones. Watch your partner's body language, mood, interaction, and conversation anytime you introduce your family members. From your observation, you can detect if your partner accepts your family or not.

Make the most of every feedback you receive. Remember: you don't want a spouse that tortures your loved ones. God commands us in Exodus 20:12. "*Honour your father and your mother, that your days may be long in the land that the Lord your God is giving you.*" You honour your parents by showing them love, care, respect, and support. Marry someone who will promote these values and more in your life because marriage should increase your ability to perform your godly duties. Don't go to the altar with a partner that will dishonour your family and loved ones. It will unleash problems in your marriage.

Family relationship is important. Thus don't sacrifice your family for anyone. You will regret it if you do. Ask those who renounced their family in the name of marriage. Ask them if they are happy in their marriages. The honest ones will tell you that there is a void in their lives. Many of them will tell you that they live in regret and wish that things are different. I have come across such persons. Learn from their failure. A good marriage does not destroy the values of its antecedents. It rather enhances pre-existing values.

Step Six: Proposal

This is the stage where you are prepared to be joined with your partner in marriage. At this stage, you are convinced that you can face the realities of marriage as explained in chapters 4 and 5. This is the place where you will commit your life to a particular person with God's consent. Thus, the mother of all questions pops up here: "Will you marry me?" This phrase is commonly used to propose marriage in many countries around the world. But it is a question pregnant with convictions and promises. Some of the hidden lines in "Will you marry me?" are:

- I admit that I love you endlessly and always will.
- I am convinced that you love me endlessly and always will.
- I know that you are my divinely-chosen spouse.
- I see my God-given partner and soul mate in you.
- I desire you for who you are.
- I want you to be my wife or husband.
- I want us to be for each other in marriage.
- I will be yours and yours only forever.
- I commit to stand as a worthy spouse to you.
- Come and make life worth living for me and with me.
- Come and make enduring wealth and success with me.

From the list above, you will discover that the question "Will you marry me?" is more than a fanciful cliché. It is loaded with promises and claims of eternal value. If a proposal does not reflect any of the statements above, don't make one. And don't accept one either.

Be true to yourself regarding your desires in life. Before you ask the question, or give an answer to one, think deeply. Ask yourself these questions: "Where am I in life and in this relationship?" "Do I honestly mean what I am about to say?" "Have I heard God clearly about this person?" Be at peace with yourself with these answers. "Will you marry me?" is a question that begs for truth and nothing but the truth. It is also an invitation to someone to step into the journey of your life. A proposal and its answer must, therefore, be borne out of truth encased in love. This is when the love boat is safe for a happy journey. Anything short of this suggests calamity. Once your doubts have been cleared, you can give or accept an invitation to marriage. But if you still have doubts, you should hold on the marriage proposal. Perhaps the time is not ripe for you.

The Bible says, "*One who is wise is cautious and turns away from evil, but a fool is reckless and careless*" (Proverbs 14:16 ESVi). Endeavour to resolve all confusing issues before marriage. Don't walk on thorns. The issues you ignore before marriage will haunt you in marriage. Marriage may not resolve the fears, dissatisfaction, and irritation. They may look insignificant now, but they will become magnified when you are married. These seemingly insignificant elements can create cracks in your marriage. As a result of irreconcilable differences, thousands of marriages are being dissolved across the world.

Stay safe

Play safe and stay safe. Resolve your reservations before marriage proposal. Don't assume that your marriage will fix it—whatever the "it" is. Don't sweep anything under the carpet. Be bold to confront issues, and get satisfactory answers. Don't carry negativity, reservations or regrets into marriage.

A divorced woman once told me that close to her wedding day, she suddenly felt that she was making a serious mistake by marrying her now ex-husband. She revealed that she couldn't stop to deal with her concerns before marriage. The marriage broke down within four years. And it was filled with domestic violence while it lasted. She has not been able to break away from the psychological damage she suffered decades after her divorce. If only she re-evaluated her position, if only she stopped short to sort out her concerns before her wedding!

God always warns us ahead of danger. Sometimes, the "cold-feet" we experience before we make major decisions might be the Holy Spirit pulling us by the ears to wait, step back or step aside. But we often misinterpret the signs or choose to ignore them. Either way leads to everlasting regret. To avoid regret, recognise and heed divine warnings.

You still have time to address your fears before marriage. Courtship allows you to check on those "fine prints" of your proposed marriage. Different viewpoints will be coming to you. Seek some quiet time to listen. Devote time to hear the voice of God. Have a reflection about yourself and your partner. Ponder on your feelings. Why do you have those feelings? Are they warning signals? What are these feelings trying to tell you? Are they promptings of the Holy Spirit?

Don't discard or ignore these inner prompts. They should rather serve as triggers to hear from God. Ascertain that you and your partner are compatible. And be confident that God is with you in your marital process.

God has given you the power to manage your search process. You have the power to suspend the question "Will you marry me?" or the answer to it. But if you are well-matched, move on with confidence knowing that God is with you. If you are still unsure, don't propose marriage and don't accept one until everything is clear.

Finally, the Act

A marriage proposal is often done by men while women respond to it. It is unconventional for a woman to propose to a man in some societies across the world. Men are expected to initiate the lead of this stage. They love it; they feel excited to be in charge. Similarly, women feel excited when proposed to. It is good as long as it makes both parties happy.

However, as popular as this social act is, it seems somewhat unfair against women. Any woman who proposes marriage is usually seen as desperate. When a woman proposes marriage to a man whom she loves, her action is deemed ridiculous. In my view, the notion that women are not entitled to propose marriage is sexist and repressive. Why should men hold the exclusive right to propose marriage? The woman is expected to wait until her Mr Right chooses to propose marriage. She can wait, wait and wait! If she gets the proposal, hurray! And if Mr Right never proposes, she would have waited in vain. Defeated, heartbroken and with her dreams shattered! This has happened to a lot of women, and it is still happening.

In a courtship, either of the partners should not be in a vulnerable position. To be jilted, after a long wait and particularly during courtship, can be devastating for women. And men too! The socio-psychological damage might ricochet for a very long time. If you don't want your time and expectations to be a waste, know where you stand with your partner as regards marriage. The earlier you know, the better for you.

Feel free to ask if the other party will marry you. And you can propose marriage to your partner whether you are the man or the woman. If you are a woman and you propose, it does not make you cheap. Neither does it mean you are desperate. To the wise, you place premium value on your time and safety. Smart people protect themselves against unpleasant surprises. You don't need time-wasters in your life. And the simplest way to know if your partner will marry you is to ask: "Will you marry me?"

The Responses: Yes, No or Maybe
In today's world, the question "Will you marry me?"

receives different responses from "yes" to a slap. I have seen a couple of videotapes on social media about these different responses. While some girls leap for joy and hug their would-be spouses, others assault theirs. The younger generation, in particular, has numerous surprising antics. And it is good. But no question warrants violence or rudeness. God gave us an invaluable piece of advice in Colossians 4:6. *"Let your speech be always with grace, seasoned with salt, that ye may know how ye ought to answer every man."* A grace-filled speech cannot be rude or violent. The appropriate response should simply be, "Yes, I will." Or "No, I can't" or simply "Maybe!" Any of these three possible answers depends on your decision to have the proposer as your spouse. Your response should be about you, not anyone else.

Let's review the three possible answers to a proposal.

(1) YES: This response means you will marry the proposer and remain the proposer's partner forever. Say "Yes" only when you are convinced that you want the proposer as your spouse. It will determine your marriage. Therefore, say "Yes" to a marriage proposal when you know beyond doubts that the proposer is your God-given partner.

(2) NO: Say "No" when you are convinced that you have no future with the proposer. Say 'no' when you cannot see a happy role for you and your children in the relationship. If you have followed the recommendation in this book to this point, you will know if the partner is yours or not. Be confident to say "No!" And let your "No" be "No." Don't

give in to any form of manipulation once you have made your position clear.

This particular response might bring an unexpected and sad end to your courtship, but it is a bold one. It may also be liberating for you as it compels you to end a relationship that might not bring happiness in the future. A broken heart at this stage is repairable. If God guides you to say "No" to a proposal, He has a better marriage for you.

(3) MAYBE: This answer is not popular. You hardly hear anyone say that to a marriage proposal. Yet, it is a positive and frank answer like a "No" or "Yes." If you are not sure of what to say, reply with "maybe" and mean it. It plainly communicates what it means: I may or may not marry you.

This answer gives you and your potential spouse the opportunities to:

1. Review your positions
2. Work on restraining factors
3. Agree on a date to come back to the marriage proposal

Clearing your doubts before marriage is to your mutual advantage. A very good friend of mine confided that when her ex-husband proposed to her, she had doubts about their future together, but she dismissed them as cold feet. She did not want to disappoint her mother who had grown fond of her would-be husband and had consequently encouraged her to accept his proposal. She became a victim of domestic abuse as soon as they got married. The demon in the husband had come home to roost. The daily torture left her with a mental scar. And three years later, they were divorced.

The Holy Spirit will warn you ahead of danger. And you will be saved from a bad marriage if you obey. On the other side of the coin, if you propose and get a "maybe," don't be discouraged. It is not the end of courtship. It only calls for patience and prayers. Try to understand the cause of the hesitation. Discuss with your partner and mentors. Above all, pray to God for help. Psalm 45:1 assures that *"God is our Refuge and Strength, a very present help in trouble."*

When I was growing up, I heard my dad said many times: "I don't take a 'no' for an answer." I didn't really know why he would utter those words. But over the years, as I reflected on the dynamic attitude of my dad, I realised that it was his way of saying he was prepared to walk through difficulties if he had to, to get what he wanted. He was not a quitter. God expects us to be persistent in our search. He will strengthen us to endure difficulties before we attain our possessions.

God has not made us quitters but winners. And we are more than conquerors through Jesus Christ that strengthens us. Don't be discouraged if you don't get the expected "Yes" to your proposal. Rejection is not a failure unless you elevate it to be one. So it should not stop you from searching. Any "no" or "maybe" that you receive suggests that there are hurdles you need to cross before you can obtain your possession. Quitters don't win laurels. Thus don't let a "No" or "Maybe" dampen your spirit. If you have to move to a new pasture, do that.

Step Seven: The Last Lap

This is the stage where you fulfil your engagement promise and agree on your wedding plans. You must stay focused because this is the most delicate stage before marriage. Marriage is a spiritual journey towards what God has ordained for you. Thus, it is not unusual for human and spiritual forces to fortify their opposition against your marriage. They will try to stop you from possessing God's provisions for your life. This ominous plot makes this stage susceptible to strange conflicts between partners. Watch out for unnecessary arguments. Strange opposition against your marriage might come from family members, friends, and other loved ones. Either of you might have fears. You might face sexual temptations from people, some of whom are from your past relationships. This agenda is to stop you from getting married. Don't give in to these forces. Many people abruptly ended their promising relationship without a good reason. Some even failed to turn up on their wedding day. They got so close but were stopped from tasting the joy of marriage. This shall not be your story.

In this last lap of your search, always turn to God. God has already given you victory over all powers and principalities that want to toil with your joy. Put on the whole armour of God to withstand every device against your marriage. Be on your guard. Fast and pray to God to see you through this process and lead you into marriage. And God will help you. He will guide your steps. God will stop you from giving in to ill-advice, unholy offers, and temptations. He will erase your fears about marriage. You should also be careful about sharing your marriage plans with the world, particularly on social media.

Avoidable self-affliction

You are in the final lap of your marital search, and this stage calls for spiritual astuteness. A lot of people forget this easily as they focus on wedding plans rather than marriage. You are not yet married, so don't conduct yourself as one. This may sound strange, but you should note that you have only made a promise to marry your partner.

Those who lose sight of this position often misbehave. They let down their guard and are influenced by lust. Some engage in cohabitation, living together as though they were married. They engage in premarital sex and even bear children out of wedlock. They make a mockery of marriage as instituted by God. The consequences of these actions are often devastating. They lead to problems in marriage, premarital breakups and divorce.

Don't run ahead of God. You started your search with God; it is important that you stay with Him. His ordinances should override every carnal urge. Stay away from sin if you want to reap the blessings of a godly marriage. Until you take the marital vow before God and an army of witnesses, you are not yet married.

The second dimension of the last lap before marriage is to watch out for godly qualities in your spouse. Share your expectations with your partner. Marriages thrive on collaboration. Work together with your partner before and after marriage. Communicate effectively, and consider each other's suggestions. Harness your knowledge and goals to forge a common plan for your future. A marriage where spouses cannot work together will collapse. And many marriages have fallen into pieces due to this aberration.

As you watch out for external forces against your marriage, you should also watch out for differences that may ruin this stage. Both of you should consider the quality of your decisions. Watch out for your judgement and emotions while you discuss subjects such as:

- Marriage date.
- Wedding plans .
- Cost of wedding.
- Cost of living.
- Where to live.
- Sex and sexual behaviour.
- When to have children.
- The number of children.
- Church to attend.
- Career.
- Money-making and saving plans.
- Relationship with friends and relatives.

Other mundane things might come up. They will challenge your judgement and stretch your reasoning. You must listen with patience, discuss objectively, negotiate, and decide. Seek knowledge and godly advice. In everything, ensure that you jointly work things out and take the best course of action.

At this stage of your marital journey, you should always recall that *"Love is patient and is kind; love doesn't envy. Love doesn't brag, is not proud, doesn't behave itself inappropriately, doesn't seek its own way, is not provoked, takes no account of evil; doesn't rejoice in unrighteousness, but rejoices with the truth; bears all things, believes all things, hopes all things, endures all things. Love never fails..."* (2 Corinthians 13.6-8) If your relationship does not reflect this nature of love, there is a problem. And you can both fix it if you follow God's instruction.

Remember that you are two individuals with different perspectives on life. Individual differences are not necessarily destructive; what often destroys is the mismanagement of these differences. Differences can be converted into strength. But your differences must not oppose biblical values or your aspirations. You and your partner must eliminate negative differences before you take the marriage vows. Don't allow your differences to cast a dark cloud over your marriage. It might cause a devastating thunderstorm.

Today, many marriages are in ruins because of differences between spouses. Courts often pronounce marriages dead on grounds of "irreconcilable differences." You have the duty to prevent yours from following this route. The book of Proverbs 14:16 says, *"One who is wise is cautious and turns away from evil, but a fool is reckless and careless."* If you sweep differences under the carpet, you are reckless and careless. Don't assume that you will overcome your differences in marriage. If you do, you are building your marriage on a land mine. Deal with your differences before marriage. Jointly acknowledge your positions about these differences. It will help you to know if you will go to the altar together.

Before I got married, I would often tell my wife that she should not do to me what she won't do to me in our marriage. It was my own way of telling her to be herself, without holding back attitudes that I might find questionable and unacceptable in our marriage. And I lived up to the same demand as well. This step was to help us see that we could live together happily.

In your final run, dot the *i's* and cross the *t's*. If after all your effort and collaboration, you noticed warning signals, think twice before you marry. It is better to be temporary hurt in courtship than be permanently sorry in marriage.

Orderliness

The seven steps enumerated above are meant to organise your premarital activities. Sadly, a lot of people do not follow the process step by step. They muddle up the steps. They confuse themselves by taking courtship stance while still at the friendship stage. Some even hurry through the whole stages. Don't allow anyone to decide the timespan of your pre-marriage journey except God. The world has cultures and religions that don't allow would-be couples to meet and know each other before their wedding. An example of such is an arranged marriage.

You should spend quality time to walk and work through all the steps enumerated above. By doing so, you will build your marriage on a firm foundation.

Guiding Light

See to it that no one takes you captive by philosophy and empty deceit, according to human tradition, according to the elemental spirits of the world, and not according to Christ
(Colossians 2:8 ESVi).

The soul of the sluggard craves and gets nothing, while the soul of the diligent is richly supplied
(Proverbs 13:4 ESVi).

11
PERSONAL GROOMING

*Let no man despise thy youth; but be thou an
example of the believers, in word, in conversation,
in charity, in spirit, in faith, in purity.*

—1 Timothy 4:12

The best of our abilities does not necessarily qualify
us for the best of God's provision. We need God's
grace to possess and keep His blessings. We can
only possess the best of possessions in joy, including a
glorious marriage, through the grace of God. However,
we must prepare ourselves to receive what belongs to us.
This act of self-preparation is what I tag *personal grooming*.
After all, marriage is not for boys and girls, but men and
women who are well-groomed.

Popular Grooming
As an undergraduate, I went around the campus with two
major items in my pocket: a comb and handkerchief. They
were my first grooming kits. I hated a sweaty and an oily
face, which were then and are still common to many

people living under the blazing West African sun. My Afro must stay tidy. My shoes and the collar of my shirts were always clean. These and more were aimed at something: girls. It sounds silly today, but back then, it was what "fine-boys" did. We never wanted to appear sweaty or unkempt before our female counterparts. The '70s and '80s were years when West African boys won girls' admiration through their dress sense. And we dressed well! You would be a public joke if you appeared rough. On hindsight, some of us became obsessive with looking good. Spending long hours before the mirror, we would beat up our Afro and repeat it many times a day with combs. We gave pimples no chance of survival on our young faces. We would use charcoal and salt to wash our teeth to maintain the whiteness. The "fine boy" appearance was our priority. And yes, it worked! It got us noticed and gave us girlfriends.

The same thing still goes on today. Young men and women focus on their outward grooming. The objective and style may be different, but personal grooming is the major investment of many young people today. Looking good is perhaps much more alive among the youths today than it was in the past. Good clothes, shoes, bags, cosmetics, etc. are the order of the day. The young ones spend resources on hairstyling, teeth whitening, manicure and pedicure, good clothing, weight shedding, etc. Many unmarried people, including my own children, are in the swing of this trend. And they double their effort when marriage comes into the equation. There is nothing bad in identifying with this. In fact, it is great if you do.

You must always look attractive, and I won't hesitate to recommend this for anyone in search of a spouse. Make an effort to look good. On a general note, a good appearance attracts people. The easiest way to be barred from respectable social circles is to be unkempt. Unwashed clothes, smelly mouth, coloured teeth, dirty nails, unkempt hair, scruffy shoes, etc. do not appeal to people. In your search for your spouse, your appearance is weighty. It is your first selling point. Your packaging precedes you, and it must promote you. It should attract the kind of person you will like to marry. Naomi handed this wisdom to Ruth with regards to Boaz when she said: *"Wash, put on perfumed oil, and wear your best clothes. Go down to the threshing floor, but don't let the man know you are there until he has finished eating and drinking"* (Ruth 3:3 CBS). This is still relevant today. It worked for Ruth, and it will work for you.

Do It Appropriately

In your attempt to look attractive, refrain from anything that will compromise your dignity as a child of God. The fashion world and social media are corrupt and will encourage you to "flaunt it if you have it." Nowadays, you'll see indecency in the name of dressing. God, knowing that we will face this situation today, had forewarned us: *"Do not let your adorning be external – the braiding of hair and the putting on of gold jewellery, or the clothing you wear – but let your adorning be the hidden person of the heart with the imperishable beauty of a gentle and quiet spirit, which in God's sight is very precious"* (1 Peter 3:3-4). My understanding of this admonition includes the fact that God calls us to moral decency. Work towards being much more beautiful on the inside than on the outside.

In the bid to appear attractive, many unmarried undergo cosmetology, tattooing, and plastic surgeries. Some ended in regrets and permanent damage. But you don't have to reconfigure your appearance in order to get the right partner. Have confidence in God, and rest in the truth that you were created wonderfully. (See Psalm 139:14)

Keep Yourself Safe

There is more to your appearance. If you are serious about enjoying your future and bringing up your children in a happy home, you will look beyond the physical appearance of your would-be spouse. Outward appearance without a well-groomed heart is lethal. A handsome man does not equate a suitable spouse. Likewise, a woman's beauty does not qualify her for marriage. God's word puts this truth in a very blunt manner: *"As a ring of gold in a swine's snout so is a beautiful woman who lacks discretion"* (Proverbs 11:22).

To use Jesus' description in Matthew 23, many people are like whitewashed tombs which look beautiful on the outside but on the inside are full of dead men's bones. They are snakes in sheep's skins. They project falsehood. Don't lust after people's physical attributes when you don't know their stand in God. Look beyond the veil; don't settle for deceptive images. Keep yourself safe so you won't be deceived. Uncover the person behind the good looks. Six–pack abs don't make a potential husband. Beautiful clothes and designer shoes don't equate peaceful marriage. Botox and cosmetics may create good looks, but the made-up face might become your worst nightmare.

Jezebel is a perfect example. The Phoenician princess and wife of King Ahab took delight in her cosmetics. She loved to look sexy and queenly. In her last hours of life, she still gave attention to her looks, styling her hair and applying makeups. (See 2 Kings 9:30.) But behind Jezebel's physical beauty was a calculated and cold-blooded murderer. Ultimately, her evil deeds brought destruction to her and her entire household. Therefore, look beyond the flesh. Don't be captured by the outward appearance. Divine formation should be the basis of your choice, not makeup.

Are You Fit?

Now, let us flip the coin and focus on you. Have you considered your heart and spirit? Do you measure up to the person you claim to be? Are you healthy for quality human relationships such as a marriage? Are you fit for marriage? If you honestly desire a successful marriage, you ought to ask yourself these pertinent questions. Don't deceive someone into marriage.

We all have flaws that wage war against us. These

flaws may hinder us from growing into the best version of ourselves. We call them personal weaknesses or bad habits. Some are outright bad behaviours that we struggle with secretly. If you carry out a critical self-audit, you will find shortcomings that pose risks to your marriage. Deal with them before marriage. Give no room to any hidden flaw. This is what effective personal grooming is all about. Failure to remove clogs in marital search can frustrate your effort. To avoid this, deal with your weaknesses.

Guiding Light

See io it that no one takes you captive by philosophy and empty deceit, according to human tradition, according to the elemental spirits of the world, and not according to Christ.
(Colossians 2:8).

I praise you, for I am fearfully and wonderfully made. Wonderful are your works; my soul knows it very well.
(Psalm 139:14).

12
YOU NEED TO KNOW HOW

Let us draw near with a true heart in full assurance of faith, with our hearts sprinkled clean from an evil conscience and our bodies washed with pure water. — Hebrews 10:22 ESV

Many unmarried men and women are aware of hidden problems that can destroy relationships. And they are good at hiding them. They also know that these problems can destroy their home. Consequently, they are afraid of going into a relationship. With their struggles staring them in the face, they tell themselves that marriage is not for them. They tell limiting lies, similar to the ones identified in Chapter 9 of this book.

By holding on to lies, they deny themselves the opportunities of promising relationships and marrying the right person. If you are one of such, you need help. Simply acknowledge your problem and understand that your case is not helpless. There is no weakness — doubt, low self-esteem, guilt, fear, pride — that cannot be overcome. God has given you victory over weaknesses. And your victory is assured through personal grooming.

Grooming The Inside

How can you groom your mind? How do you prepare your mind prior to finding your spouse? How do you become fit for your role as a spouse?

(1) *Know who you are*: It starts with knowing who you truly are. If you know that you are a child of God, you will act like one. The Spirit of God will dwell in you richly and righteousness will be your watchword. You will be heaven-focused in your relationship and marriage. You will have a distaste for iniquity. Unholy thoughts will not have dominion over you, and you will be strong enough to abstain from immorality and lies.

(2) *Be Well-Grounded in Faith:* Premarital grooming requires you to be well-grounded in faith. We live in a time where the word of God is being compromised on many fronts, including marriage. You must know the truth about marriage. Attend Christian seminars on marriages. Participate in relationship-building programmes. Read good Christian books and e-books on marriages. Search the Scripture daily and understand marriage doctrines. Listen to sermons and counsels by pastors, spiritual mentors and bible-minded parents. *"Children obey your parents in the Lord: for this is right. Honour thy father and mother; which is the first commandment with promise; That it may be well with thee, and thou mayest live long on the earth"* (Ephesians 6:1-3). Here it is again! The health and wealth of your marriage can be determined by how you treat the instructions of your spiritual guides.

(3) *Be filled with the Fruits of the Holy Spirit:* Once you are well-groomed for marriage, you will manifest the fruits of the Holy Spirit. You will become loving, peaceful, joyful, forgiving, enduring, meek, honest, and trustworthy. You won't delight in *"Acts of the flesh... sexual immorality, impurity and debauchery; idolatry and witchcraft; hatred, discord, jealousy, fits of rage, selfish ambition, dissensions, factions and envy; drunkenness, orgies, and the like"* as stated in Galatians 5:19-22 (NIV). If you still exhibit any of these sinful behaviours, repent and turn away from it because taking it into marriage is dangerous.

I try to put God first in all of my thoughts and actions. And I have enjoyed continuous success, joy, and blessing in life. I encourage my children to acknowledge God in everything they do. I always remind them that God is omniscient. He knows, sees, and judges all things. Thus, it is important that they keep themselves acceptable before God. I also encourage them to abstain from sin and uphold the virtues of Christianity. They are to stand for the truth at all times and remain compassionate towards all. They must boldly resist every evil manipulation. These and many more are efforts towards my children's formation and personal grooming.

I am happy that there are many Christian parents, guardians, friends, and pastors who are daily moulding the character and minds of those in their care. We want them to become whom God has called them to be. Success, on this beat, includes well-groomed men and women. You must be equipped with the character that supports love, respect, and unity in marriage. As the fruits of the Holy Spirit grow in you, rest assured that you are set for a happy marriage. According to the law of attraction, likes attract likes. You will attract persons that share your faith and spirit — the exact stock from where your spouse will emerge.

In Urgent Need of Grooming

If you lack the fruits of the Holy Spirit but desire a happy marriage, you have urgent work to do. Start grooming yourself in the way of the Lord today. Give your life to Jesus Christ. Ask the Holy Spirit to help you. Ask God to make you a new creature. David, a man after the heart of God, did that when he cried out: *"Create in me a clean heart, O God, and renew a right spirit within me"* (Psalm 51:10). You should do the same. If there is any sin in your life, ask God for forgiveness. Don't run after your pursuits with a sinful heart. Seek God's intervention and run away from sin.

In the presence of God, the greatest inadequacy of man is smaller than the smallest speck on earth. Nothing is impossible for Him to fix. There is no irredeemable situation before Him. He can deliver us from every bondage of addiction, generational curses, sexual immorality, lies, anger, depression, fear, confusion, poverty, etc. But we need to allow Him by going on our knees to ask for His help. We must surrender all to Him if we want to be well-groomed for a happy marriage.

If there is anything that will ruin you or your marriage, turn it into God's hands. You know your struggles and weakness better than anyone. Seek help from God. And be prepared to surrender all to Him. Accept Jesus Christ as your Lord and Saviour. Seek assistance from mentors and prayer partners. You may need to start reading the Bible. Download Bible apps on your phone. Listen to the word of God. Faith comes by hearing and hearing through the word of God. (See Romans 10:17) When you do all of these, your mind will be renewed.

You are stronger than your challenges, so don't give in to temptation. Challenges need your compliance to pin you down. But if you don't comply, you cannot be destroyed. Refuse to be taken into captivity. Don't surrender to any form of unrighteousness. Stand firm in God if you desire a glorious marriage. You are a pillar in your marriage. As a pillar, you must be fit for support. But you can't do this without God. A broken pillar is hazardous to a building. So don't be a broken pillar lest you put your marriage in danger.

With personality defects, you will struggle to find and keep a spouse. The Bible advises us: *"Let the thief no longer steal, but rather let him labour, doing honest work with his own hands, so that he may have something to share with anyone in need"* (Ephesians 4:28). Bad behaviour will disqualify you for marriage. Examine yourself today; identify loose ends in your life and tidy up. Allow God and spiritual mentors and coaches to help you. And grow daily into a better version of yourself. This is the heart of personal grooming; it is a prerequisite for attracting the right spouse.

Guiding Light

*Therefore, beloved, since you are waiting
for these, be diligent to be found by him
without spot or blemish, and at peace*
(2 Peter 3:14 ESVi).

*Wash yourselves; make yourselves clean;
remove the evil of your deeds from before
my eyes; cease to do evil, learn to do
good; seek justice, correct oppression;
bring justice to the fatherless, plead the
widow's cause*
(Isaiah 1:16-17).

13
CONCLUSION

*That which we have seen and heard we proclaim
also to you, so that you too may have fellowship
with us; and indeed our fellowship is with the
Father and with His Son Jesus Christ.* — 1 John 1:3
ESVi

On July 18th, 2017, my wife and I were on a flight to Chicago O'Hare International Airport, U.S.A., from Reykjavik Airport, Iceland. An hour into the flight, we noticed the cabin crew serving meals to some passengers. We anxiously awaited ours but nothing came. The serving crew had skipped us to hand out meals to other passengers. We called a member of the cabin crew to inform them that we have not been served. She politely told us that we were not entitled to any meal. We were shocked! We were not going to eat on an almost seven-hour flight? Of course, we quickly demanded why. With the same politeness, the air hostess told us that the tickets we paid for online had no provision for meals. We were dumbfounded. She must have noticed our shock when she added, "We can give you water if you want." By this time, my wife was upset and did not hide her disgust from the air hostess.

As frequent international flight passengers, we have never encountered anything like this. We also would never have expected an international flight, such as Iceland Air, to "starve" any of its customers. We did not think that the ticket we paid for was a low-cost or budget flight service. We told the air hostess all of these and more! The air hostess calmly explained that the information was on their website where we had obtained our tickets. We muttered in frustration, concluding that we would never fly Iceland Air again. All of these changed nothing. There was no meal for us.

However, it dawned on me that Iceland Air was not at fault. We have not been treated unfairly either. We missed a vital piece of information while procuring the tickets online. So we were responsible for getting the flight tickets that did not entitle us to meals. We created this discomfort for ourselves in our long journey to the US. We, not the Iceland Air, made that decision – though inadvertently. Unfortunately, we could not reverse it there and then. We were to live by the choice that we made. We watched others ate and drank around us. But we ate too. God made a way for us. My wife had stuffed some plantain chips in her hand luggage. She has the habit of keeping snacks in her hand luggage anytime we travelled. This time, the snacks came to our rescue. We munched the plantain chips at different times to fight off hunger until the flight lasted.

There are three moral and spiritual lessons I learnt from this experience. And they are relevant to the title of this book.

1. In life, it is easy to make errors that have grave consequences. Errors can disqualify us from a school game, affect our academic grades or cost us job opportunities. They can make us miss our bus rides or arrive late for our flights. Errors, made out of ignorance or impatience, can come back to bite when we least expect.

2. Sometimes, we fail to pay attention to details. We ignore small prints. We don't notice the danger signs on the roads we travel. We ignore hints of caution and miss great opportunities because they appear insignificant.

3. When the consequences of our omissions show up later in life, they leave us devastated and regretful. But with God, we can find comfort.

Every journey requires adequate preparation. You must pay attention to detail and small prints. Confirm that you meet all the requirements for a smooth journey. Cross checking the details of your journey before departure is crucial. All arrangements for a successful journey must be in order before the journey. Proverbs 21:5 ESV reveals that *"The plans of the diligent lead surely to abundance, but everyone who is hasty comes only to poverty."*

Marriage, as described in this book, requires the same degree of diligent pre-planning. It requires commitment to the details — small prints — about your choice of spouse. It also involves dealing with any hidden disqualifier in you. But your checking system cannot be carnal. It must be spiritual and kept so. Don't be moved by emotions or sight. Rely on the help of the Holy Spirit. Push aside your own thoughts, and allow God to lead you. The Scripture reveals that the heart of men is desperately wicked and unpredictable. It warns us not to lean on our understanding but to trust in the Lord with all our heart. Therefore, don't give room for your heart to lead you astray.

As you prepare for marriage, you must commit your life to God. Marriage can make or destroy you; you need God to get it right. Allow the Holy Spirit to dictate every step you take towards marriage, not the social media, new-age culture or emotions. The way to bring this to fruition has been presented in this book.

It is my desire that you enter into a marriage where you will find fulfilment — a marriage where you and your spouse will remain thankful to God. Go into a marriage that will delight your children, parents, relatives, friends, and acquaintances.

You deserve peace and happiness at every stage of your marriage. The earlier you start this process, the better for you. Start the search process today. Fine-tune your understanding about marriage. Appreciate the uniqueness of your spouse. Identify God's interest in it, and commit your ways to Him. Don't marry without God.

I pray that the Lord will bring you into a fruitful union

with the bone of your bone and flesh of your flesh. I pray that He will bless your path and make your way prosperous. It shall be well with you and your marriage. I pray this day that the Spirit of the Lord will rest upon you as you search for your spouse. His Spirit of wisdom will take you to the right places. The fear of God will rule over your choice of a spouse. And you shall find favour with God. All these and more I pray for you today in the precious name of our Lord Jesus Christ. Amen.

Guiding Truth
The Lord is at hand; do not be anxious about anything, but in everything by prayer and supplication with thanksgiving let your requests be made known to God. And the peace of God, which surpasses all understanding, will guard your hearts and your minds in Christ Jesus.
(Philippians 4:4-7 ESVi)

Wishing you a successful Journey

Printed in Great Britain
by Amazon

59426004R00088